Athens

...

A guide to recent architecture

Errica Protestou

Athens

A guide to recent architecture

● ● ● ellipsis KÖNEMANN

•••

CREATED, EDITED AND DESIGNED BY
Ellipsis London Limited
2 Rufus Street London N1 6PE
E MAIL ...@ellipsis.co.uk
WWW http://www.ellipsis.com
PUBLISHED IN THE UK AND AFRICA BY
Ellipsis London Limited
SERIES EDITOR Tom Neville
EDITOR Annie Bridges
SERIES DESIGN Jonathan Moberly
LAYOUT Pauline Harrison

COPYRIGHT © 1998 Könemann
Verlagsgesellschaft mbH
Bonner Str. 126, D-50968 Köln
PRODUCTION MANAGER Detlev Schaper
PRINTING AND BINDING Sing Cheong
Printing Ltd
Printed in Hong Kong

ISBN 3 8290 0470 2 (Könemann)
ISBN 1 899858 55 5 (Ellipsis)

Errica Protestou 1998

Contents

Introduction

This is the first guide to be devoted exclusively to the architecture of the Athens/Attiki region. When I began writing it, I felt that there were only a few ways to go about it. One way would have been to be ruthlessly choosy and include only the buildings I like – daring but hardly practical, and not representative of Athens at all. Another way would have been to go to the other extreme, to accept established opinion of what is considered great architecture and be done with it – but that would be too easy and, again, it would not tell the reader much about Athens. The hundred or so schemes that I have decided to include, therefore, are not just the ones I like, but also those that show the influences and development of Greek architecture whether good or bad – in effect, presenting the city as it really is. This means that in some instances there may be just a single entry from a well-known architect compared to two or three from a relatively unknown colleague.

This introduction is not intended as a summary of the history of Greek architecture, but it will take you briefly through the major factors that have influenced the development of Greek architecture and made Athens what it is today.

The guide itself covers a cross-section of public, residential, industrial and commercial projects not only by well-known architects but also by young rising stars – proving that there is indeed life after the Parthenon. The earliest projects I have included date back to the 1950s, when Greece was trying to come to terms with the effects of the Second World War and the civil war of 1947–49 – events that had destroyed some 400,000 of the country's buildings.

The period of prosperity and rapid economic development that began in 1952 under a right-wing government was initially expressed through large-scale road construction throughout the country. Between 1950–60 the demographic pattern of Greece changed as the rural population deserted the countryside for the cities. This wave of migration worsened the housing shortages in the cities, particularly in Athens. But the Government, preoccupied with the regions that had suffered most heavily during the civil war, and with the island areas that had been shattered by the disastrous earthquakes of the 1950s, passed the housing problem into the hands of private businessmen. They in turn developed the system of part-exchange known as *antiparohi* whereby land for building is acquired from its owner in exchange for an agreed number of apartments in the finished scheme, plus little or no capital.

Demand alone could never have developed and shaped a building production line of the scale, dynamism and flexibility of the system of part-exchange. The limited fluidity of the economy and the lack of funding for the construction of houses led to its consolidation. Eventually, the system covered the construction not only of housing but also of office blocks and other work spaces, and even holiday resorts. Many building firms and builders provided labour in exchange for housing. But – because of the small property sizes, the restrictions of the building regulations and the contractors' desire to achieve maximum profit – the result was low-quality architecture.

The *antiparohi* system encouraged the standardisation of the apartment block and is responsible for the way Athens looks today. It led to the use of materials that were easily available and construction methods that were simple and could be carried out by unskilled labour. Concrete proved to be the most appropriate material for such a basic form of construction and met virtually every architectural demand. However, very little care was taken with the quality of the construction of the concrete frame since it was invariably covered with some sort of coating

Athens: a guide to recent architecture

or cladding. Only when the look of exposed concrete and propping by columns became popular did new advanced methods appear.

The success of the *antiparohi* system created a boom in the building industry that lasted until the mid-1960s, and apartment blocks spread rapidly throughout Athens: 520 of them were built in 1960, for example, compared to 68 in 1950. Inevitably, this rapid development caused the destruction of many important 19th-century neo-classical buildings – a situation made worse when, to disguise this tremendous loss, parts or materials from neo-classical buildings were incorporated into new structures – with hideous results. A few efforts were made to restore some of the neo-classical buildings, mostly by the owners, but had little effect.

Despite the low quality of its architecture, the city-centre apartment block became something that was aspired to by those who could not afford one and who lived in older two- or three-storey buildings in poor neighbourhoods, or in the country. At the first opportunity, these people made the façades of their own homes look like fragmented or smaller versions of the city-centre apartment blocks: colour zones over the lintel, standardised balcony railings and metal entrances were some of the features used to achieve this result.

Amid all this chaos, a new type of client emerged, one who had survived the war and who sought reassurance in the safe, familiar styles and theories of the past. At the same time, architects were also turning towards the past, searching for the Greek character in architecture. Somehow, the symmetry and simplified classical elements that were generally considered 'Greek' were no longer in evidence in the Athens apartment block, which had been reduced to a concrete box (it was not until 1951 that its form was renewed, with Nikos Valsamakis' apartment block on Semitelou Street).

The first large-scale building of the post-war era was the Athens Hilton (built between 1958 and 1963, see page 24), which soon became a symbol of foreign investment in the city, and a morphological prototype for monumental architecture. The architects for the Hilton project had been faced with a dilemma: what architectural language should they use – American or Greek? They ended up with a widely accepted 'international' solution: an arrangement of public spaces on the ground level, through which the main volume, accommodating the private spaces, is shot through. The façade of the latter, facing on to the street, had no openings – something unthinkable for those days – though the Greek Pentelikon marble used for the façade and the atriums (both of which made reference to the Parthenon) and the extensive planting of olive trees were reassuringly Greek. Coincidentally, the design of the US Embassy (see page 18), built at around the same time, used similar features – features that would henceforth be regarded as an expression of formal Greek architecture. What everyone failed to notice was that many American buildings of that era shared the same arrangement and features: the architecture of Mies, Stone, Johnson and others was being imposed in Athens under the pretext of having a Greek character.

It seemed that inevitably, eventually, Greek architecture would align itself with Western architecture. The growing economy, increasing industrialisation, the greater numbers of students enrolling in architecture schools, the broadening of the architect's social role, the circulation of international and local architecture magazines, the overseas training of many architects – all these factors contributed to the promise of a 'new' architecture. The influence of brutalism, the Bauhaus, Le Corbusier and Mies was apparent in the 1960s, especially in architectural competitions.

The most important representative of Greek post-war architecture was

Aris Konstantinidis who, as head of OEK (the organisation for working-class housing) between 1955 and 1957, applied socialist ideas to the building of housing: a house, he believed, should cover the material, emotional and psychological needs of the individual; it should add to and complete a composition of houses, streets, gardens, hills, mountains and sea. Konstantinidis' ideas were expressed through exposed concrete frames which followed a grid determining the exterior and interior form of the houses, and also through the use of primary colours for the walls. The use of colour was such an important issue for Konstantinidis that, when OEK insisted on only white buildings, he left to work for the Tourist Board (EOT). He felt that traditional Greek architecture was, and should continue to be, multi-coloured. His transfer to EOT saw the continuing 'Hellenisation' of the basic principles of modernism.

Other, younger architects such as Nicos Valsamakis and Takis Zenetos dared to ignore completely the issue of Greek character, thus liberating Greek architecture from its links with the past. Valsamakis, while innovative, never designed buildings that were provocative to the general public. But he approached the typology of Mies and Neutra in a bold manner; his architecture helped to renew Greek architecture and place it in an international context. Zenetos was an extremely talented architect who refused to adapt or compromise, constantly challenging the theoretical and technological standards of architecture in Greece. Eventually he took his own life, but he remains an example of what might have been achieved had conditions been right for him at the time.

Alongside this younger generation of architects came Dimitris Pikionis, whose projects included the Acropolis paving and the masterplan for the Loubardiari area (1951–57). Pikionis' approach was to integrate his designs into the landscape with the minimum possible intervention, as if the design had always been there, untouched by human hand, part of nature. Parallels have been drawn between his work and the Japanese respect for the landscape.

Soon attempts were made to record and research all these new approaches to architecture. As well as the pan-Hellenic architecture conventions there came various magazines such as *Architecture in Greece*, *Zygos* and SADAS (though these tended to eschew real criticism).

Visiting Athens to look at its modern architecture can be a disappointing experience today, especially for the foreign traveller who has had visions of the Acropolis drummed into his consciousness. In that respect, Greeks have a lot to live up to. Nevertheless, Athens continues to develop slowly and steadily, with many brave, small-scale interventions, and a walk through the city can prove very refreshing (if a little chaotic) if approached in the right frame of mind. Attention to detail is definitely required because – due to the lack of technological and financial backup – the buildings are not spectacular or beautiful in an obvious kind of way. There are no impressive high-tech skyscrapers or wide, clean boulevards. There isn't even a proper infrastructure – if it rains for long enough the city floods.

There is a general air of confusion too, with some architects still searching for 'Greekness' and others faithfully following or even copying the various international architecture movements. Economic recession and the corruption that accompanies some design-and-build packages only add to the confusion. Unfortunately, as a result, what eventually gets built in Athens is rarely representative of what is really going on in the Greek architecture world. There is a lot of talent about, as one can see by glancing at invaluable architecture magazines such as *Tefchos*, or by looking at the many competition entries by Greek architects. A guide to

Athens: a guide to recent architecture

the unbuilt competition entries would perhaps have been a more appropriate way to show what the younger generation is capable of.

ACKNOWLEDGEMENTS

Thank you to all the architects who so generously supplied photographs, drawings and other material; to Orestis Doumanis, Kalliopi Kontozoglou and Yiorgos Simeoforidis for their guidance; to Tom Neville for giving me the opportunity to write this book; to Christopher Davy for his love and generosity; to my co-sufferer Christina Muwanga for her friendship, encouragement and sound advice; to the Papasavvas family for their tireless support; but most of all to my mother and best friend for her unconditional love. It should be noted that for the introduction to this book I drew on *Modern Greek Architecture* by Dimitris Philippidis, published by Melissa, and *Housing in Greece – a Crisis in the Production Relations*, published by the Foundation of Mediterranean Studies.

Athens: a guide to recent architecture

Using this book

This guide is broken down into the 16 geographical sections that make up Athens, Attiki (Greater Athens) and the coast including Euboea. Each section can be covered on foot apart from the coast and Euboea areas. Addresses are listed for each entry, though some of the street numbers have been excluded for security reasons. The nearest bus or trolley stop is also listed. Where the cost of a scheme is included, this is given in drachmas and refers to the year that the building was completed.

Bus and trolley services in Athens are extremely cheap, and a flat fare will take you to any part of the city (though these days you may have trouble finding standing room, let alone a seat). Special ticket booths and some kiosks near bus stops issue multi-packs of tickets that can be used on both services. Tickets should be inserted into the orange automatic machines as you get on to the bus or trolley and retained until the end of the journey for inspection by plain-clothed inspectors. Bus numbers change, so always double-check before you set off. Completion of the Athens metro has been delayed by the discovery during construction of archaeological ruins, but it will hopefully be finished by the end of the century. If the weather is not too hot, Athens is also a wonderful city for walking, especially around Plaka where you can catch great views of the Acropolis.

If you cannot bear the hustle, take a taxi. Taxis in Athens are cheap – an average fare costs around 500 drachmas depending on traffic during the day, or double that after midnight or on bank holidays. It is customary to share taxis, so be prepared (it is against the law to carry more than four persons, so it won't be too much of a squeeze). Taxis are usually hailed in the street; make sure you are standing on the right side of the road to hail a taxi heading in the direction you want to go, and shout out the area you want as it goes past – it is easier than it sounds. Taxis can be pre-booked for a small charge.

If you can read Greek the Kapranidis/ELPA map is recommended, otherwise get the Michelin one.

Athens: a guide to recent architecture

Vasilissis Sofias, Kolonaki, Academia

US Embassy

The tight security measures surrounding the embassy add to the general air of hostility that it projects. The use of a grid system and the building's square-within-a-square form, row of columns and controlled landscape make up the basic language of this pompous composition. An obscure colonnade around the main building was developed in response to the intense Athenian light.

The embassy was built at around the same time as the Athens Hilton (see page 24), which employs a similar architectural language. Both schemes came to be seen as symbols of foreign investment and as morphological prototypes for monumental architecture (see introduction).

ADDRESS Vasilissis Sofias Avenue
COLLABORATING ARCHITECT P A Sakellarios
BUS A5, 450, 550 TROLLEY 3, 7, 8, 13
ACCESS none

Walter Gropius/TAC 1961

Vasilissis Sofias, Kolonaki, Academia

Walter Gropius/TAC 1961

Megaron Musices (concert hall)

Built along the same lines as the Supreme Court (see page 94) – to create an imposing aura – this white, symmetrical, austere-looking building has become a landmark in the city and a cultural centre for musical and other artistic events. A visit to the concert hall is recommended.

Construction started in the 1970s but was soon interrupted. When it restarted seven years later, it was felt that the original Keilholz-Vourekas scheme was out of date in terms of the building's acoustic and technological requirements. Extra facilities were added to the brief, including recording studios, conference rooms and exhibition spaces.

Vasilissis Sofias, Kolonaki, Academia

ADDRESS Vasilissis Sofias Avenue
COLLABORATING ARCHITECTS
P A Sakellarios, E Tzanetatou,
Elias and Nikos Kavoulakos,
K Kourousopoulos, A Irving,
G Graikos, P Heliotis
ACOUSTICS Skroubelos and
K Opitz of Muller BBM
CONSTRUCTION GEK SA and
Psyctiki Hellas SA
BUS 450, 550, A5
TROLLEY 3, 7, 8, 13
ACCESS open

Keilholz-Vourekas, Kyriakides, Scholides, Sgoutas, Skroubelos 1975

Keilholz-Vourekas, Kyriakides, Scholides, Sgoutas, Skroubelos

Parametros offices

The brief called for the design of offices for a large contracting company for food products. The interior design of the spaces was accomplished without demolishing the existing walls or altering the structure of this 1950s fifth-storey apartment. Three new spaces were created – a conference room, a work room and the director's office – as well as an external, tent-like metal construction to shade the terrace.

To avoid fragmentation into small rooms and labyrinthine corridors, a floating ceiling (of timber sheets painted yellow, with spotlights) was devised to cover the whole area. This linear element penetrates both rooms and corridors, unifying them as well as subtly defining circulation.

In the extremely small conference room (which has spectacular views over Lycabettus Hill), above-eye-level mirrors reflect the floating timber ceiling, thus creating the illusion of a much larger space and preventing it from becoming claustrophic.

The conference table – a glass, ship-shaped top resting on a bright-blue metal construction – is a reference both to the company's technical competence and the naval forms much loved by the director.

An entrance hall featuring a sand-blasted door and a magnified engraving of Archimedes' hydraulic timepiece separates the offices from the rest of the working spaces.

ADDRESS 66 Vasilissis Sofias Avenue
CLIENT Parametros
COLLABORATOR Nicos Constantopoulos
ASSOCIATE DESIGNER D Skouroyiannis
SIZE 75 square metres
COST 5 million drachmas
BUS A5, 408 TROLLEY 7, 8, 13 ACCESS limited

Elias Constantopoulos 1994

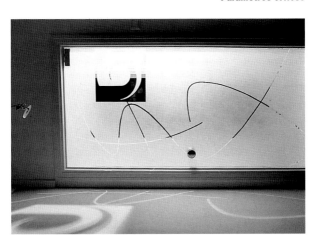

Elias Constantopoulos 1994

The Athens Hilton

This hotel was the subject of great debate when it was built because of its positioning and size, which were regarded as offensive: 54 metres high, its size went against the building regulations of the time, (though these were subsequently altered by the planning department). Before the erection of the Hilton, the Parthenon monopolised the Athens skyline and was the only building that could be seen at a distance from the city.

Several photographs and sketches of the two buildings were published in the American magazine *Architectural Forum*, in an article which portrayed the hotel's modernism as offensive since it had the audacity to compete not only with the Acropolis (along its southern axis) but with ancient Greek history as a whole.

Vasilissis Sofias, Kolonaki, Academia

ADDRESS Vasilissis Sofias Avenue
CLIENT Athens Hilton
FAÇADE G Pappas
ADVISORS Warner, Burns, Joane, Winde
BUS 408, 450, 550, 601, 603, A5 TROLLEY 3, 7, 13
ACCESS limited

M Vourekas, S Staikos, A Georgiades, D Vlassis 1963

Vasilissis Sofias, Kolonaki, Academia

M Vourekas, S Staikos, A Georgiades, D Vlassis 1963

The National Gallery

The National Gallery, almost т-shaped in plan, comprises two independent buildings connected by a bridge. It includes galleries for the display of sculpture, paintings and engravings, an outdoor display space for sculpture, a lecture hall, reception area, administrative offices, library, workshops, storage and utilities. The design was required to fulfil three requirements: to separate temporary and permanent exhibition spaces (yet allow vertical communication between them); to provide the largest possible outdoor space; and to set the whole scheme back from the street (with direct or visual access to the gardens).

The building, which was the winning entry in a competition held for the project, exudes a sense of importance.

Vasilissis Sofias, Kolonaki, Academia

ADDRESS 50 Vasileos Konstantinou Avenue
COLLABORATING ARCHITECT Dimitris Antonakakis
BUS 550
TROLLEY 3, 7, 13
ACCESS open

M Vourekas, S Staikos, A Georgiades, D Vlassis 1963

The Athens School of Music

For financial reasons, the Athens School of Music constitutes the only part to be built of an original, larger scheme. Its form — a very long white slab with equally long, semi-enclosed corridors (often used by local kids for skateboarding) — accommodates all the facilities in a row. The conservatory contains 35 classrooms, a rehearsal hall for opera and drama, an exercise room, seven staff offices, a music museum, a library, a concert hall, an auditorium and a chapel.

The scheme was the winning entry in the 1959 Athens Cultural Centre planning competition.

ADDRESS Vasileos Konstantinou Avenue and Regillis Street
BUS 450, 550
ACCESS open

J Despotopoulos 1976

Vasilissis Sofias, Kolonaki, Academia

Vasilissis Sofias, Kolonaki, Academia

J Despotopoulos 1976

Corundum

Do not walk into this precious stones shop expecting to see the products on display – concealment is the focus of the architects' design. Security measures are cleverly incorporated, without arming the premises to the teeth or giving them a fortress-like appearance. The use of the Latin word *corundum* (meaning 'precious stone') adds to the shop's air of secrecy, as does the architects' decision to conceal the safe, contrary to common practice.

Corundum is for wholesale customers only; their casually asking to see samples will enable you to see its anonymity disintegrate before your very eyes. Nothing too much is revealed too quickly — just the odd glimpse of a 15-centimetre-thick door or tiny wooden panels (which had appeared to be merely decorative) opening up to divulge beautiful stones. Things are not what they seem in this shop, which is otherwise minimally decorated with Greek marble and African wood.

Vasilissis Sofias, Kolonaki, Academia

ADDRESS 17 Kalamiotou and 5 Skouze Street, Syntagma
CLIENT Corundum
SIZE 100 square metres
COST 20 million drachmas
TROLLEY 3, 7, 13
ACCESS limited

Takis Koumbis and Katerina Karanikou 1993

Vasilissis Sofias, Kolonaki, Academia

Takis Koumbis and Katerina Karanikou 1993

German Embassy

The German Embassy was conceived as a prominent building responding to its challenging corner site. To emphasise this corner situation a curtain wall serves as a background to a golden sphere which rises and descends in a 12-hour rhythm, almost carving off the corner of the building.

The architects separated the six-level building into four zones based on function: mechanical, representative, office and recreation. The interiors are very much shaped by the architects' idea of a modern office space. Each floor has a distinct colour, expressed on the staircase landings and the round stucco columns in the corridors. White is the main colour for the interiors, complemented by Greek-blue elements, a patterned carpet and ample lighting.

The building combines Greek traditional materials with modern technology in an attempt to slow down its deterioration in the polluted Athens atmosphere.

Vasilissis Sofias, Kolonaki, Academia

ADDRESS Ipsilandou and Karaoli Demetriou Streets
CLIENT The Federal Republic of Germany
ENGINEERS Pagonis, Chroneas, Kinatos
CONTRACTORS MBN, Hanover and Fintias SA, Athens
SIZE 3000 square metres
TROLLEY 3, 7, 13
ACCESS none

Senkowsky Sakellariou Architects & Town Planners 1993

Vasilissis Sofias, Kolonaki, Academia

Senkowsky Sakellariou Architects & Town Planners 1993

Museum of Cycladic Art

This museum was designed to house the exceptional and much travelled N P Goulandris Collection of Cycladic Art, which drew a quarter of a million visitors when it was on loan to the Washington National Gallery. Only the National Museum in Athens has a collection of Cycladic antiquities that can compete in range and quality.

The glass and marble four-storey building in the city centre has three display floors: one for the Cycladic works, another for ancient Greek art from the period between 2000 BC and 400 AD, and a third for temporary exhibitions. There is also a children's display area, an auditorium, a cafeteria, and a museum shop selling low-priced copies of the figurines.

The display and lighting of the 200 or so items was a difficult task as the figurines, pots, marble vessels and metalware of the Cyclades are small and need to be viewed up close. Both tasks have been carried out in a striking, beautiful and minimal way by the two Americans responsible for the design of the exhibition in Washington, whose skills Mrs Goulandris had admired.

Vasilissis Sofias, Kolonaki, Academia

ADDRESS 4 Neophytou Douka Street, Kolonaki
CLIENT Goulandris
DISPLAY AND LIGHTING G Anson, E Quenroe
ACCESS open Monday, Wednesday, Thursday–Saturday 10.00–16.00, closed Sunday and Tuesday; tickets 400 drachmas (free Saturday)

J Vikelas 1985

J Vikelas 1985

Vasilissis Sofias, Kolonaki, Academia

Armando Moustaki

This small *faux bijoux* shop is in the most exclusive shopping area of Athens. The original shop was designed in the 1980s by the architect George Triantafyllou, and derives its image and morphology from the early metro stations of Athens – hence the small wagon-like compartments and ceramic tiles.

The brief called for the alteration of half the shop in order to accommodate more merchandise. A simpler, more up-to-date version of the train now forms a new wall. Semi-translucent curved Perspex and varnished MDF display windows add to its subtle and gentle appearance.

Vasilissis Sofias, Kolonaki, Academia

ADDRESS 7 Xanthou Street, Kolonaki
CLIENT Armando Moustaki
ASSOCIATE D Skouroyiannis
COST 5 million drachmas
BUS 022, 60
ACCESS open

Elias Constantopoulos 1994

Elias Constantopoulos 1994

Helen B clothes shop

In the most affluent and prestigious area in the centre of Athens, this shop stocks mainly the DKNY line of clothing. A service slab in the middle carries the changing rooms and toilets, dividing the space in two. The area given over to women's clothing has a wooden floor running throughout the length of the shop. Lit from underneath and lifted off the ground by 15 centimetres, it appears to be floating, creating a softer, more feminine environment. Clothes are displayed and moved along metal tubes in front of a sand-blasted wall which is lit from behind.

The men's clothing area has an untreated granite floor and a changing room that is an integral part of the slab. The 1.8-metre-high slab has an overhanging glass roof which folds at a right angle and stops just before it reaches the floor, creating a space where customers can look in the mirror before leaving the changing room.

Worth visiting.

LOCATION at the end of Anagnostopoulou Street, Kolonaki
CLIENT Helen B
SIZE 150 square metres
COST 40 million drachmas
BUS 022, 60
ACCESS open

A Van Gilder, B Ioannou, T Sotiropoulos 1993

Vasilissis Sofias, Kolonaki, Academia

A Van Gilder, B Ioannou, T Sotiropoulos 1993

Astrolavos art gallery

This gallery, which occupies the first four levels of a typical Athens apartment block, emerged out of the demolition of the previous one, with design decisions taken on site due to the shortage of time. The staircase and walkway are used to create a route through the gallery, almost carving out and marking the edges of the space. The main exhibition area is on the lower ground floor, with smaller exhibition spaces on the upper ground floor and in the basement.

The architect has succeeded in designing a gallery where exhibits can be comfortably displayed without losing their identity.

Vasilissis Sofias, Kolonaki, Academia

ADDRESS 11 Xanthippou Street, Dexameni, Kolonaki
CLIENT A Dimitrakopoulou
SIZE 350 square metres
COST 140 million drachmas
BUS 022, 60
ACCESS open Tuesday–Friday 10.30–14:00, 18.00–21:00; Saturday
10.30–14.00; closed Sunday and Monday

Solon Xenopoulos 1994

Solon Xenopoulos 1994

Sina Street furniture shop and offices

This flagship store, part of a chain, is tucked away in a narrow street in the centre of Athens, where its carefully lit façade catches the eye of passers-by in the evenings. Kontozoglou explains how the idea of using a mask on the façade came about: 'In *Rashomon*, Kurosawa tells a simple story three times, describing the events from three different viewpoints. All three narratives are "true", even though they differ from each other. In the theatre, the mask releases the actor from the obligation to use his face, allowing him to give himself over completely to the spoken word and body movement. It also releases the audience from the need to observe detailed expressions, permitting absorption of the event as a whole. The office block in Sina Street is a similar case. In order to achieve transcendence, the design of the elevations made use of a "mask" of reinforced concrete. The archetypal office block, in the form of a "glass box", conceals within itself a concrete frame while at the same time concealing itself behind a concrete mask.'

Vasilissis Sofias, Kolonaki, Academia

ADDRESS 11–13 Sina Street, Kolonaki
CLIENT Varangis
ENGINEERS F Zoeopoulos and A Zaimis
CONSTRUCTION Theta Delta Building SA
SIZE 2680 square metres
BUS A5, 022
ACCESS open

Dimitris Varangis and K Kontozoglou 1993

Vasilissis Sofias, Kolonaki, Academia

Dimitris Varangis and K Kontozoglou 1993

French Institute extension

The French Institute is situated on a corner site in the centre of Athens. The corner is emphasised with the presence of an eye-catching, single-storey carved wall.

The architect's intervention consists of a 400-seat amphitheatre on the ground level and classrooms on each of the upper two levels. The size of these spaces can be adapted according to need, providing either six or eight classrooms. In addition there are chemistry and photographic laboratories, office spaces and a hostel.

Vasilissis Sofias, Kolonaki, Academia

ADDRESS Sina Street, Kolonaki
CLIENT French Institute
ENGINEERS V Vavaroutas, I Leloudas
COST 20 million drachmas
BUS A5
ACCESS limited

Demosthenis Molfesis 1973

Demosthenis Molfesis 1973

French School of Archaeology administration building

Until the 1960s, when it was decided that the existing building did not satisfy the school's growing needs, the French School of Archaeology had occupied an old neo-classical building set in a large garden. A modern separate administration building was then erected in a corner of the garden, leaving as much space as possible around the old premises (now used as a library and accommodation for archaeologists). Apart from offices, the administration building incorporates a house for the security guard, laboratories, drawing rooms and spaces specifically designed for the filing of drawings and rare books.

This small, modernist structure is characteristic of Tsolakis' perfectly resolved, simple, functional approach – in this case influenced also by the difficult financial conditions in Greece at the time.

Vasilissis Sofias, Kolonaki, Academia

ADDRESS Didotou and Sina Streets, Kolonaki
CLIENT French School of Archaeology
SIZE 950 square metres
BUS A5, 60
ACCESS limited

Panos Tsolakis 1962

Panos Tsolakis 1962

Lykavitos offices and residence

The structure took advantage of its steep transversal site by opening up to the street on two different levels. Two offices on the lower levels and a residence above develop around a west-facing garden. The three levels of the residence expand and become part of private horizontal spaces without affecting each other's identity. Various elements carry this gesture through. The double-volume living room, which is circular in plan, uses its courtyard properties to join and re-order spaces. The transition from one to another – by means of large openings, different lighting and subtle changes in direction – blurs the boundaries of each space and adds to its plasticity.

Vasilissis Sofias, Kolonaki, Academia

ADDRESS 4 Dafnomili and 3 Leontos Sgourou Streets
CLIENT Bouki Babalou-Noukaki and Antonis Noukakis
ENGINEER Costas Agapiou
SIZE 523 square metres
COST 50 million drachmas
BUS A5, 450
ACCESS none

Bouki Babalou-Noukaki and Antonis Noukakis 1995

Bouki Babalou-Noukaki and Antonis Noukakis 1995

Didotou Street apartment block

The decision of the contractor, landowner and architect to move away from the conventional apartment block design (which in most cases results from the part-exchange system of building, see introduction), led to a vertical development of individual houses over two or three levels at a time. All dwellings have 2.5-metre-high spaces extending around a central 4-metre core. Various transitional levels are reflected on the building's façade as protruding elements and cavities. The parapets — a classic mid-war feature — make reference to the neighbouring housing block, whereas the height of the building and the triangular balconies unite the block with the neo-classical building next door.

The ground level, accommodating a row of shops and the main entrance, acts as an extension to the pedestrian street, making it the focal point of the neighbourhood.

ADDRESS Didotou Street, Kolonaki
ENGINEER/CONTRACTOR John Demopoulos
SIZE 950 square metres
BUS A5
ACCESS none

Vasilissis Sofias, Kolonaki, Academia

Alexandros Patsouris 1991

Alexandros Patsouris 1991

Zografou to Paleo Falero

School of Philosophy

For a panoramic view of this building take the peripheral that passes through Katehaki Street and head out towards the airport. Because of its small site, the School of Philosophy is densely built and has few open spaces. The amphitheatres are separated from the main building, whose volume is broken down into smaller parts. In contrast to the School of Theology (see page 56), it is an inward-looking building, with a multi-storey interior passage which acts as a social gathering place.

The passage starts at the main entrance; located along it are a large amphitheatre, a students' materials shop, a refectory and a two-storey atrium covered with glass pyramids and surrounded by lecturers' offices. The atrium acts as an icon and as a navigation point from other areas of the building.

Colour is used to define circulation; and to make it less confusing, all corridors and stairs lead off the interior passage.

A walk through the School is like a journey through the history of philosophy, with the various workshops evoking different periods.

Zografou to Paleo Falero

ADDRESS Panepistimioupolis, Goudi, Zografou
CLIENT University of Athens
ENGINEERS Pagonis, Chroneas, Kinatos and A Panos
SIZE 35,000 square metres
COST 1 billion drachmas
BUS 220, 221
ACCESS open

L Kalyvitis, G Leonardos, A Zannos, P Tsolakis 1982

Zografou to Paleo Falero

L Kalyvitis, G Leonardos, A Zannos, P Tsolakis 1982

School of Theology

The School of Theology was the winning entry for the University of Athens competition. It was designed to take advantage of the hillside site and is arranged in parallel zones of different heights, connected by corridors. These links subdivide the open spaces between the zones, creating peaceful courtyards where students can meet and relax. There are essentially four zones: the first contains the main entrance, dean's office, secretary's office, library and museum; the second zone houses four amphitheatres and a leisure area; the third accommodates workshops; and the fourth contains lecturers' offices and four Institutes.

The simple and restrained appearance of the school results from a monastery-like spatial arrangement and features from the Byzantine period such as the vaults used in the Institutes and lecture halls. The architects had to struggle with a tight budget and therefore used very basic materials.

Although a University church was part of the competition, it was never built – because of financial but mainly aesthetic concerns.

Zografou to Paleo Falero

ADDRESS Panepistimioupolis, Goudi, Zografou
CLIENT University of Athens
ENGINEERS Pagonis, Chroneas, Kinatos
SIZE 11000 square metres
COST 50 million drachmas
BUS 220, 221
ACCESS open

Lazaros Kalyvitis, George Leonardos 1965

Lazaros Kalyvitis, George Leonardos 1965

Linea Nuova

This furniture shop in Pangrati is an example of what can be achieved with a rented space – on an extremely tight budget and in a simple but effective way. Although the materials used were mainly MDF and 'Novopan', aesthetics were in no way compromised. All interventions were limited to the interior of the shop.

Furniture is tastefully displayed on raised platforms – of three different heights – in front of a two-storey wall which acts as a backdrop. The most interesting features of the shop are the three-dimensional shapes which emerge from the walls, carved to form spaces for individual pieces of furniture.

ADDRESS 8 Formionos Street, Pangrati
CLIENT Linea Nuova
BUS 550
ACCESS open

Katerina Valsamaki

Katerina Valsamaki

House in Pangrati

Built in the early 1960s, this four-level house is one of the finest examples of Konstantinidis' smaller private projects. The site's size and odd shape – an irregular pentagon/prism – influenced the design of the street elevation and the arrangement of spaces. The elevation is formed by two triangular volumes that intersect each other to accommodate the master bedroom and the music room on the third and fourth levels, high above the street to ensure privacy. All the spaces are arranged vertically, with subsidiary spaces on the lower two levels. The use of intersecting volumes, together with the spread of spaces over four levels along a diagonally positioned axis, breaks up what would otherwise be a very narrow façade and monotonous plan.

Zografou to Paleo Falero

ADDRESS corner of Archimidous and Kleitomahou Street
BUS 450, 550
ACCESS none

Aris Konstantinidis 1962

Zografou to Paleo Falero

Aris Konstantinidis 1962

Zannas residence

This house for a pianist, a writer and their two children is situated on a quasi-pedestrian street. Its overall volume was determined by building regulations, in particular by a requirement to provide free space at the back and by a height restriction of 8.3 metres.

The house was conceived as a home/work environment, where various activities unfold from sunrise to sunset. To reflect this continual activity throughout the house, spaces of diverse heights interpenetrate each other, and materials gradually change to follow a predetermined itinerary. A simple construction elaborated in order to reveal an underlying rhythm.

Zografou to Paleo Falero

ADDRESS 17 Pinotsi Street, Philopappou
CLIENT Zannas
ENGINEER G Monemvasitis
SIZE 400 square metres
BUS 150
ACCESS none

Atelier 66 (D and S Antonakaki) 1972

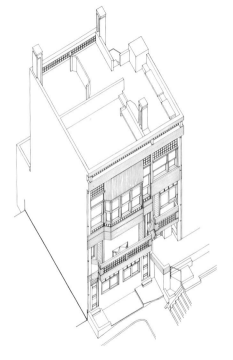

Atelier 66 (D and S Antonakaki) 1972

Artist's studio and residence

The house is situated in a traditional residential area, on a slope between two streets, facing the historical cliff of Philopappou, near the Acropolis. Its restricted site was an inducement to extend the height of the building, which is on four main levels above a courtyard. The courtyard addresses the street and also provides secondary access to the house, as was often the case in late 19th- and early 20th-century Athenian houses, a number of which can still be found in the area.

The first two levels of the building accommodate the studio and the remaining ones the living spaces. A freestanding stairway incorporating a hydraulic lift shaft serves as a visual and functional connection between the levels. The shaft, a structural element made out of red-coloured steel sections, is itself an interesting feature, with its moving cabin acting as a unifying element in space.

ADDRESS 17 Arakynthou Street, Philopappou, Acropolis
CLIENT Elias and Maria Dekoulakos
ENGINEERS Yannis Tsopanakis, George Diamantouros
SIZE 400 square metres
COST 24 million drachmas
BUS 150
ACCESS none

George Makris and Argiris Rokas 1984

George Makris and Argiris Rokas 1984

Nea Smyrni apartment block

Most apartment blocks in Athens are of low quality, mainly because they are built for part-exchange (a system that gives rise to many difficulties, see introduction) and because of the contractor's desire to achieve maximum profit.

Here, however, the architect decided to treat the contractor's demands and financial restraints as a challenge. The requirement for better lower-zone flats was satisfied by improving their relationship with the street and the open spaces. This was achieved by giving them a separate entrance (accessed through the back garden) and changing the hierarchy of enclosed/semi-enclosed spaces, the size and type of balconies, and so on. The best-selling 95- and 115-square-metre flats were rearranged and used to create a new morphology for the whole block, without having to be reduced in size. In this way the individuality of the flats was maintained.

The architect successfully answered the challenge by designing an apartment block that dealt directly with all the demands: lower zones were made available to the land owner and the higher, more expensive, zones to the contractor, as a bonus. Thus, both parties were satisfied.

ADDRESS 4 Thali Milesiou Street, Nea Smyrni
CLIENT S Diamantis
ENGINEER G Kestebekis
SIZE 800 square metres
TROLLEY 10
ACCESS none

Panos Kokkoris 1991

Zografou to Paleo Falero

Panos Kokkoris 1991

Nea Smyrni Square

A road forms the edge of this slightly sloping rectangular area. Its pavement, decorated with large reinforced-concrete tiles, sets the mood. The surface of the pavement is treated with colour, texture or pattern before it is dry. This hands-on approach ensures that nothing is geometrical, repeated or static, and emphasises the rough and outdoor character of the environment in an artistic, elegant way.

Today the square is unfortunately a bit run down, but one can still tell that at one time it was a beautiful synthesis of three main elements – concrete, earth and water – moving under and over each other to form bridges, gaps, barriers and different levels that emphasise the natural slope of the site. The main attraction for passers-by is the sound of recycled water moving through the square, pumped out or thrown from its highest point to the lower levels, forming a series of ponds along the way.

Zografou to Paleo Falero

CLIENT Municipality of Nea Smyrni
ENGINEERS Gregory Kathetzopoulos, Spyros Pavlides
SIZE 10,000 square metres (200 x 50 metres)
TROLLEY 10
ACCESS open

Lazaros Kalyvitis, George Leonardos 1969

Lazaros Kalyvitis, George Leonardos 1969

Orthopaedic consultancy

This converted flat is the successful result of an attempt to provide maximum effect with minimum intervention, since the existing space did not offer many possibilities. The idea was to confront the existing walls by covering them with new layers of wood and glass which would unify the disparate spaces into a continuous whole. These new walls serve for the most part as shelves. With their warm hues of mahogany and rosewood, and with the indirect light from the glazed areas, a warm ambience has been achieved. The furniture, made out of interlocking planes and protruding and sculpted elements, creates a game between doctor and patients.

In the waiting room an undulating bookcase incorporating a similarly curving sofa slides along a luminous glass bubble that contains the kitchen, cuts the edge of the marble sink, and permits glimpses of a semi-exterior space. In the examining room the many inlays and divisions create separate areas of use, assisting the doctor in his work.

Zografou to Paleo Falero

ADDRESS 56 Raidestou Street, Nea Smyrni
CLIENT Katsifarakis
SIZE 80 square metres
COST 12 million drachmas
TROLLEY 10
ACCESS limited

Nicos Constantopoulos 1992

Zografou to Paleo Falero

Nicos Constantopoulos 1992

Comprehensive school

Four collaborating schools with a total of 2000 children make up this high school community. The unfortunate choice of materials and colours does not do the building justice. The scheme is organised around a system of atriums that develops along a dominant axis which also serves as the main passage and outdoor space. This system forms the boundary between the private areas of each school and the large public spaces. The administration, library, gymnasium and multi-use hall are open and are regarded as an independent zone serving the neighbouring community.

ADDRESS Vouliagmenis Avenue, Ilioupoli
CLIENT Ministry of Education
ARCHITECTS T Biris, D Biris, M Kafritsa, T Papaloannou, I Karakostas, D Nikiforaki
COLLABORATORS (COMPETITION) I Karakostas, D Nikiforaki, N Toulatos, E Frangopoulou (students)
BUS A3
ACCESS limited

Various 1988

Various 1988

Aghios Dimitrios secondary school

The school accommodates 1500 students over three identical levels and was designed around a circular nucleus containing the audio-visual department. The staff offices and classrooms were placed in direct contact with this central element, thereby reducing building costs, corridor circulation and the number of supervisory staff required. In addition, polygonal layout meant that large open-air areas were preserved. In order to minimise costs even further, the design permits partial or complete prefabrication, fixed elements are durable and involve a simple construction method, and movable elements are low cost and disposable.

The building can adapt to new developments in teaching methods and equipment by a simple extension of its facilities, and it can also be replicated in other locations. Built in the 1970s, it is still the most powerful modern building in Athens.

Zografou to Paleo Falero

ADDRESS Papagou and Thrassyvoulou Streets, Aghios Dimitrios
BUS 111, 219
ACCESS limited

Takis Zenetos 1976

Takis Zenetos 1976

Flisvos Square and waterfront landscape sculpture

Nella Golanda, a sculptor, has sensitively designed the overall layout, furniture and surfaces of Flisvos Square with the intention of liberating its sea view.

The seats, made out of wood and various stone elements set on concrete and stone bases, frame the central spaces of the square. Their form, flowing with the space rather than intruding, triggers the imagination with its various levels and un-seat-like shapes. The central area reuses old stone slabs, with grey and white decorative panels highlighting entrances and crossways.

The waterfront landscape sculpture, executed four years later, constitutes a natural extension to Flisvos Square, following its rhythm until it reaches the sea. The sculptural, multi-level, angular seats invite their users to enter into a particular relationship with the landscape. The sculptor once wrote: 'Sometimes they feel as if they are seated in boats similar to those sailing around the quay ... or sometimes, when the weather is good and the mountains of nearby Aegina Island are visible, they can relate their shape to the square's forms and benches ... at other times, when the sea is rough, the rhythm of the waves seems to represent a succession of white marble and cement.'

ADDRESS Poseidonos Avenue, Paleo Falero
CLIENT Municipality of Paleon Faliron
SIZE square 2.5 hectares; sculpture 0.75 hectares
BUS 133, A2 to Flisvos
ACCESS open

Zografou to Paleo Falero

Nella Golanda 1982 and 1986

Fokionos Negri to Ampelokipi

Velvet Café

Velvet Café is on a busy pedestrian street with a large number of other cafés and bars. It unfolds over three levels – the basement accommodates preparation areas, offices and toilets; the ground floor has a seating area, bar and DJ area; and the first level provides extra seating.

The aim was to create a vibrant environment that would attract the younger generation by standing out from the rest of the cafés in the area. The composition is based on contrasting materials and colours. Thus cold materials were used for the floors (tiles, grey granite and rusty-brown marble), the equipment (stainless steel) and various elements including the railings (metal and stainless steel). As a contrast, warm colours and materials were used for the furniture (wooden chairs and leather sofas), the bar, the shelves and the DJ area.

A journey through the space is achieved by means of a freestanding metal staircase that leads from the double-volume entrance hall through a wooden link to the wooden first-floor extension. The journey is made more pleasant by different coloured lighting. The café's furnishings, however, are disappointing.

ADDRESS 15 Fokionos Negri Street, Kypseli
CLIENT Chrisostomos and Vangelis Tassis
SIZE 220 square metres
COST 70 million drachmas
BUS 022, 622 TROLLEY 3, 13, 14
ACCESS open

Nikos Lykoudis, Ismeni Papaspiliopoulou 1993

Fokionos Negri to Ampelokipi

Aeriko Café

On one of the busiest pedestrian streets, this slick café/bar is on two levels, with two separate bars, a seating area on each level and a DJ space on the ground floor. The mood of the café is set by the juxtaposition of contrasting materials and colours: the hardness of marble and steel co-exists with the warmth of wood, the roughness of plaster counterbalances the smoothness of stucco antico, and rough grey marble emphasises the smooth curves of the orange roof.

Coloured lights add another dimension to the café's mood. Six neon lights shine through glass holes in the ceiling, brightening the ground floor. In the evening, a specially lit metal façade, with crystal treated to give a shattered-glass effect, creates countless shades of colour and adds an air of mystery.

Fokionos Negri to Ampelokipi

ADDRESS 25 Fokionos Negri Street, Kypseli
CLIENT Chrisostomos and Vangelis Tassis
SIZE 200 square metres
COST 60 million drachmas
BUS 622 TROLLEY 3, 13, 14
ACCESS open

Nikos Lykoudis, Ismeni Papaspiliopoulou 1994

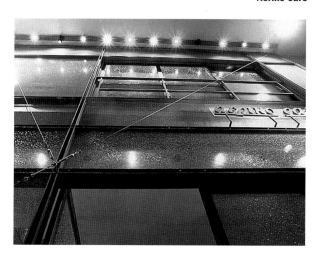

Fokionos Negri to Ampelokipi

Nikos Lykoudis, Ismeni Papaspiliopoulou 1994

Souvatzidis office and residence

The architect is best known for his design of solar housing using the Balcomb method and the Solarsat computer program. He has applied this knowledge to his own home/work environment, together with a more romanticised idea of what a home should be like – a reflection of dreams, memories and emotions that involved himself and the surrounding area.

The combination of different openings to important views and the desire for maximum use of solar energy led to angular cuts and elements which are set back or protrude from the façade, sometimes painted gold in order to reflect the light.

Best of all is the playful and imaginative way in which the architect has recycled old, discarded materials, creating installations and sculptures which speak out against consumerism and capitalism. Note the huge metal 'guardian angel' at the entrance.

ADDRESS 15 P Yalourou Street, Attiko Alsos
CLIENT M Souvatzidis
CIVIL ENGINEER T Gogos
MECHANICAL ENGINEER S Apostolopoulos
SOLARSAT PROGRAM S S Tsioutsias and D B Grintzias
SIZE 500 square metres
COST 50 million drachmas
BUS 450, 550, 610
ACCESS by appointment with owner

Michael Souvatzidis 1993

Michael Souvatzidis 1993

Mytaras solar residence

This award-winning solar house was designed by a leading expert in the field, Souvatzidis, with the help of the SOLARSAT computer program. Situated on a hillside, it is home to a talented family of two painters and a musician.

Through the use of passive solar design elements in the sections and plans, the shell of this building is determined by both the course of the sun and the functions of the interior spaces. Apart from assuring thermal gain, this has the advantage of creating complex elevations and inner arrangements. There is a studio on each of the three levels of the house, designed specially to suit the needs of the artists and to stimulate the imagination. The introduction of an interior garden on the bedroom level brings to mind Greek island houses and gives a feel of traditional Greek architecture to an otherwise modern city dwelling.

Fokionos Negri to Ampelokipi

ADDRESS 15 Kamariotou Street, Nea Filothei
ENGINEER T Gogos
SOLARSAT PROGRAM S S Tsioutsias and D B Grintzias
TILES handmade by Vernardaki
SIZE 405 square metres
COST 15 million drachmas
BUS 610, 450, 550
ACCESS none

Michael Souvatzidis 1985

Michael Souvatzidis 1985

Bakou Street apartment block

The structure was developed over four levels, with each of the three apartments occupying more than one floor. In this respect it differs from the usual 'flat per floor' arrangement of most apartment blocks in Athens. Thanks to their elevated situation, the flats enjoy magnificent views of the hill nearby and the rest of the city.

Cavities and protruding elements on the Bauhaus-influenced front elevation alleviate the boxiness of the building and help to achieve a less austere look.

ADDRESS 57 Bakou Street, Nea Filothei
CLIENT Dimitrios Vellios
ENGINEERS Dimitrios Vellios, Antonis Frudakis
SIZE 450 square metres
COST 70 million drachmas
BUS 610
ACCESS none

Eleni Amerikanou, Panos Exarhopoulos 1995

Fokionos Negri to Ampelokipi

Eleni Amerikanou, Panos Exarhopoulos 1995

Ileana Tounta Contemporary Art Centre

The original, very basic, functional building was constructed in 1945, just after the end of the war and, with its isolated presence, has acted as a reminder of it ever since. In 1990, when the old factory was transformed into a contemporary art centre, its new use demanded 'clean' surfaces with a minimum of shadows to enable the clear display of exhibits and a diverse use of its spaces.

No radical changes were made to the existing spatial arrangements, apart from in the area near the entrance. Here, the demolition of walls and a change in levels opened up the building towards the courtyard via a multi-angled glazed opening. An open-air staircase and walkway provide a connection to the second level.

By subtly preserving the industrial feel of the original structure, the presence of the old building is allowed to re-emerge and co-exist in harmony with the new.

ADDRESS 48 Armatolon and Klefton Street
ENGINEER Yannis Tsopanakis
SIZE 610 square metres
COST 80 million drachmas
BUS 022
ACCESS open

Fokionos Negri to Ampelokipi

Eni Dimitriadis and George Drinis 1990

Eni Dimitriadis and George Drinis 1990

Alexandras Avenue office building

This commercial development by GEK and Psyktiki, two major contracting companies, stands out from the neighbouring 1930s and 1950s buildings with its modern, dark-blue metal façade. The colour of the elevation counteracts the intensity of the light that penetrates either side of this six-storey narrow building and at the same time provides a distinct aesthetic quality. The horizontal metal grilles on each level create a changing effect of multiple transparency as one moves along the street away from the building.

ADDRESS 205 Alexandras Avenue
OWNER AND CONTRACTOR GEK SA, Psyktiki SA
ASSOCIATE ARCHITECT Dina Kalamitsi
M & E CONSULTING ENGINEERS TEKEM Ltd (N Kavoulakos)
STRUCTURAL ENGINEER OMETE SA (C Kostikas, project engineer;
G Iacovidis and P Kremezis, consulting engineers)
SIZE 4000 square metres
BUS A5, A6, A7, 230, 242, 610 TROLLEY 8, 14
ACCESS none

A N Tombazis and Associates Architects Ltd 1995

Fokionos Negri to Ampelokipi

A N Tombazis and Associates Architects Ltd 1995

Supreme Court Building (Arios Pagos)

The Supreme Court Building, in the most prominent position within the Law Courts complex on Alexandras Avenue, was the winning entry in a 1969 architecture competition. Its unwelcoming façade, monolithic and austere, unintentionally creates a feeling of awe and fear. Access to this monumental building is via a large set of stairs that interrupts the rhythm of the façade. This rhythm and repetitiveness is also evident in plan, with one half the mirror image of the other.

The open-plan ground floor acts as a foyer to the levels above (housing the administrative offices and hearing chambers) and to the other buildings in the complex: the Court of Appeal, the First Instance Court, the Magistrates' Court and the Police Court.

Fokionos Negri to Ampelokipi

ADDRESS Alexandras Avenue, Ampelokipi
BUS A5, A6, A7, 230, 242, 610
ACCESS limited

J Rizos and D Kataropoulos 1980

J Rizos and D Kataropoulos 1980

Exarhia to Aigaleo

Em. Benaki Street apartment building

This block was built for four families as a co-operative venture which also involved the owner of the site. Each family has one apartment, for which they contributed a share of the capital. The building also houses the offices of the Atelier 66 practice.

Except for the second-floor unit, the flats occupy an entire floor and extend over more than one level. Although each flat has kept its individuality, some overall planning criteria were applied: visual and physical connection with the outside, cross-ventilation, and extensive use of small pockets of green space.

A very significant building even for today and a departure from the standard housing-block policy of 'one apartment per floor'.

ADDRESS 118 Em. Benaki Street, Exarhia
ENGINEERS A Athanasiades, C Dolkas
SIZE 650 square metres
COST 5 million drachmas
TROLLEY 3, 7, 13
ACCESS none

Atelier 66 (D and S Antonakaki) 1972

Exarhia to Aigaleo

Atelier 66 (D and S Antonakaki) 1972

Strefi Hill five-level building

From its position on top of Strefi Hill overlooking the rest of Athens, this two-family building with a work space on the ground floor manages to use the site's peculiarities to its advantage. The steep slope, the magnificent view and the pedestrian street running parallel to the site encouraged the development of a dwelling on five stepped levels focusing on the street. The façade follows the street line, but at ground level it is blurred by recesses and projections to accommodate the entrances, creating intermediate spaces between them and thus widening the street.

The building's exterior focuses on the pure geometry of shapes and volumes while exploring gradual changes of scale. At the same time it consciously avoids making any reference to contemporary styles.

ADDRESS 40 Poulherias Street,
Strefi Hill, Exarhia
CLIENT G Alexiou
ENGINEERS G Alexiou (civil),
S Verykios (mechanical)
SIZE 350 square metres
COST 100 million drachmas
BUS A7, 450 and a ten-minute walk up the hill
ACCESS none

Eleni Amerikanou, Panos Exarhopoulos 1990

Eleni Amerikanou, Panos Exarhopoulos 1990

Exarhia Theatre conversion

This theatre was restored with particular love and attention as it belongs to the architect's daughter. The listed building consisted of two structures: a turn-of-the-century, two-storey, neo-classical building and a later three-storey addition at the back. Its distinct narrow core, the vertical circulation along the party wall, and the development of the main areas from the street towards the back were the determining factors in the conversion's layout.

The greater part of the original building was preserved – the street elevation, the basement and ground floor, and the vertical communication core. The areas adjoining the street retained their neo-classical character, others were converted into auxiliary spaces for the theatre.

The acoustic ceiling, treated as an awning, brings to mind the outdoor performance spaces of the Middle Ages. This impression is enhanced by the use of canvas seats for the audience.

A penthouse was added over the theatre for the stage director and his family. All new parts, including the theatre itself and the penthouse, are constructed out of reinforced concrete. The street elevation was meticulously restored to its original form, except for the colour scheme. This was carefully selected with the help of Paris Prekas, a well-known Greek painter.

ADDRESS 69 Themistocleous Street, Exarhia
BUS 224
ACCESS open

Constantin Dekavallas 1990

Constantin Dekavallas 1990

Fine Arts Gallery

As you walk down this busy street in the centre of Athens, you are first introduced to the spirit of the gallery by the metal, spring-like bollards on the pavement outside. Contrary to common practice, this gallery lures its customers in and around the building by using original but subtle detailing and few openings rather than a fully glazed façade.

An unintentional change of rhythm seems to carry through the three-level building: from the business of the more socially interactive, fast-moving ground floor with its bar, garden, bookshop and exhibition space, to the slower, ideal-for-reading pace of the second floor where exhibitions continue, to the completely quiet third floor with its offices and conference rooms.

The building makes good use of natural lighting with roof reflectors and openings in the gallery space and an atrium with a pyramid-like top which directs daylight into the interior spaces.

The movement of the sun and the use of solar energy for lighting and heating the offices generated the west-facing triangular forms on the top part of the façade. Below, the exposed reinforced concrete is painted rusty brown.

ADDRESS 119–21 Harilaou Trikoupi Street, Exarhia
CLIENTS F Siantis, D Lyberopoulos
ENGINEERS J Kolmaniotis, S Apostolopoulos
SIZE 1000 square metres
COST 350 million drachmas
BUS 6, 408
ACCESS open

E Souvatzidou, M Souvatzidis 1995

Exarhia to Aigaleo

E Souvatzidou, M Souvatzidis 1995

Gnosi Bookshop/Café

The bookshop is situated in an apartment block, occupying part of the ground and first floor. It was designed in two phases: the first, in 1989, required a showroom where publishers could exhibit and sell books; the second, in 1995, called for the refurbishment of the bookshop in order to include a café.

The dark, corridor-like space with a central column made the insertion of a staircase to the upper level virtually impossible. Nevertheless, this difficulty was elegantly resolved and the problem turned into a feature. The staircase splits into two parts halfway up, wraps around the column-turned-bookcase and leads to the upper café level.

On the ground floor the bookstands, lit and suspended from the roof, use a special weight-and-pulley mechanism to display the books face on. Korres' rigorous attention to detail, combined with the imaginative spatial organisation of Kokkinou and Kourkoulas, adds a new dimension of complexity to the project.

ADDRESS 31 Ippokratous Street and Solonos Street, Exarhia
CLIENT Gnosi Bookshop
SIZE 180 square metres
BUS A5
ACCESS open

M Kokkinou, A Kourkoulas, D Korres 1989 and 1995

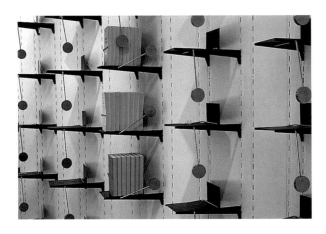

M Kokkinou, A Kourkoulas, D Korres 1989 and 1995

Metropolis music store

Metropolis, part of a chain, is the largest music store in Greece, with five floors devoted to tapes and CDs. It used to be the old 'Rossikon', the Russian patisserie famous for its *piroski,* which closed down in 1989. None of its previous function or atmosphere has survived, only its fame, the wooden roof and the 1910 metal structure, one of the first of this size in Greece.

The architects have designed a space in which it is possible to play different styles of music on each floor without creating chaos. The hard image for this store was achieved with the clever use of iron, glass, untreated stone and wood. A gigantic metal arc hanging from the façade accentuates the dramatic effect.

ADDRESS Panepistimiou Street
CLIENT Metropolis
ENGINEER Anna Borboli
COST 80 million drachmas
TROLLEY 3, 7, 13
ACCESS open

N Hiotakis, S Divaris 1991

N Hiotakis, S Divaris 1991

Ideal Cinema

The Ideal was built in 1930 and functioned as a theatre until 1965 and as a cinema until it was burnt down in 1989. It is situated between the old Athens School of Music and the Ziller building, with one of the two Ziller entrances providing access.

After its destruction, a radical space change was called for in order to accommodate the large 9 x 17-metre screen. The seats were replaced and the roof level raised by 2 metres, thus making the blank side walls even higher. The famous painter Antonopoulos came to the rescue by turning these problem areas into a feature. His series of large, dramatic, dark-grey paintings on the theme of evolution fit in well with the spirit of motion pictures. Discreetly lit, even during performances, they add yet another dimension to the cinema's atmosphere.

Exarhia to Aigaleo

ADDRESS 43 Panepistimiou Street
CLIENT Spentzos Films
SIZE 890 square metres
COST 150 million drachmas
TROLLEY 3, 7, 13
ACCESS open

Theros Architecture, V Trahanas 1990

Theros Architecture, V Trahanas 1990

General Bank

The building was formerly Flocas, a coffee shop (part of a chain), which was built in 1927 on the site of the palace's old stables and decorated in an art deco style. In 1987 it was bought out and became the headquarters of the General Bank.

As part of their intention to recreate the space as accurately as possible so that it would not look or feel fake, the architects have restored most of the art deco features and created new ones based on the original designs. To ensure authenticity, they employed the son of the carpenter responsible for the design and creation of the original coffee shop furniture. For the restoration of the 1927 shop floors specialist technicians more used to working on Byzantine churches were brought in.

The coffee shop itself, of historical importance as a meeting place for intellectuals of the time, is now transformed into the bank waiting area.

ADDRESS 9 Panepistimiou Street
CLIENT General Bank
ENGINEERS T Strangas, G Xyngogeorgopoulos
COST 125 million drachmas
TROLLEY 3, 7, 13
ACCESS open

N Hiotakis, S Divaris, D Axiotis 1987

N Hiotakis, S Divaris, D Axiotis 1987

Credit Bank headquarters

This scheme was the winner of a 1978 competition. Aesthetically, the completed version looks different, although it is based on the same concept and compositional principles as the competition entry. The intention was to portray the prestige and efficiency of the private bank through an austere and dominating design which would also be in harmony with its neo-classical neighbours.

The bank's symmetrical façade, punctuated by openings that diminish in size towards the upper levels, is a continuation of the existing street façade. The original exterior is clad with white marble panels, while the new office space above is glazed, with its recessed mass making reference to the rooflight of the adjacent neo-classical building.

The bank was constructed in two phases, the first in 1985 and the second in 1990. The central branch of the bank occupies the first basement level and the ground and first three floors; the administrative spaces are housed on the fourth to ninth floors; and mechanical plant is on the second basement level. The second phase completed the headquarters by extending the transaction areas on the ground floor, doubling the office space, adding reception areas and providing access to the underground garage.

ADDRESS corner of 40 Stadiou and Pesmazoglou Streets
COLLABORATING ARCHITECTS S Molfesis and K Manouelidis
ENGINEERS Elias and Nikos Kavoulakos, Abakoubkin and Abouselam
TROLLEY 2, 4
ACCESS open

Nicos Valsamakis 1985–90

Exarhia to Aigaleo

Nicos Valsamakis 1985–90

Tsantilis clothes shop

After purchasing the shop next door to his own, the fashion designer Tsantilis asked the architects to make the two spaces – which had three different floor sizes and no uniform identity – read as one.

The octagonal dome was replaced with a round wooden one, and all the materials of the shop were changed to achieve a new sense of direction and uniformity.

Carefully chosen materials and the existing staircase were used as devices to bring the three floors together. Towards the top, the staircase turns into marble (symbolising the sky), whereas at the bottom it is made of wood (the earth). In between, the materials (Derias, Chiou and Pentelikon marble and walnut and beech wood) are beautifully integrated and blended to bring out the order and geometry of the space.

Exarhia to Aigaleo

ADDRESS 37 Stadiou Street
CLIENT Tsantilis
SIZE 1000 square metres
BUS A2, A3
ACCESS open

I Zachariades, A Spanomarides and K Kontozoglou 1994

Ioannis Zachariades and Athanasios Spanomarides 1994

Public Power Corporation (DEH)

The Public Power Corporation was founded in 1950, but the construction of this distribution station at the junction of Tritis Septemvriou Street and Rizou Street did not come about until the completion of the PPC's electrification programme in the 1970s and Greece's attainment of technical and economic self-sufficiency.

Construction of the PPC building started in 1972 and took five years. Situated in the centre of Athens it stands out from the surrounding apartment blocks. With its unplastered concrete, aluminium-clad façades, metal door and mesh-covered windows, it is difficult to guess what its use might be. The building is a combination of symbolic and functional architecture.

Its functional design was arrived at for various reasons: the truncated triangular site on which an earlier PPC building stood; the obligation to incorporate parts of that original building; restrictions placed on the basement by the proximity of the Athens metro tunnel; and the need to install colossal new switchboards of given dimensions and adapt those that were already in place. The power distribution switchboards are recessed into two of the façades, exposing their reinforced structure, while the external surfaces of the walls are lined with flat sheets of anodised hard-alloy aluminium to improve their resistance to the effects of the atmosphere and insulate them against the direct heat of the sun.

The symbolic aspect of the design emerged from the need for a decorative element on the vertical, 2.8 by 21-metre surface that resulted from the truncation of the acute angle of the building. Krantonellis wanted an element that would portray the contemporary, technological spirit of the building. The result was a photokinetic sculpture (shamefully not in working condition today) produced with the sculptor Yorgos Zogolopoulos. It comprises a 20-metre-high column and a horizontal section

Krantonellis 1977

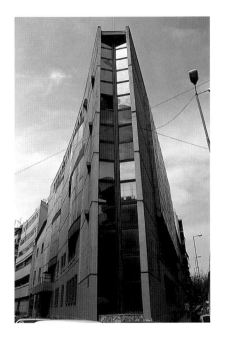

Exarhia to Aigaleo

Krantonellis 1977

made of solid glass rods. A plate placed up the entire height of the central vertical axis revolved very slowly, lit by either daylight or artificial light. Reflected in the glass rods, the plate gave the impression of masses of light passing up and down the column. Because of its prominent position on Tritis Septemvriou Street, the sculpture played an important role in the area, highlighting and symbolising the work of the PPC itself.

Exarhia to Aigaleo

ADDRESS Tritis Septemvriou Street
BUS 605, A8, B8
ACCESS none

Krantonellis 1977

Krantonellis 1977

Artist's private gallery and residence

Fasianos, a well-known Paris-based Greek artist, decided to transform his family home into small flats and a private gallery for the paintings he had kept over the years. The original structure, a neo-classical house, had been sold in a part-exchange deal and turned into a grotesque, badly built apartment block. The condition of the building, its situation in one of the most run-down areas of Athens, and the cost of preserving part of it (apparently more than demolishing and rebuilding it) did not deter the artist. To stay in the neighbourhood he grew up in, in an environment he was familiar with, was of the utmost sentimental importance to him.

The architect enjoyed a four-year process of rediscovering the building and preserving part of its structure. He likened the experience to the idea of Athens as a hidden city waiting to be discovered. Old stone walls were revealed and cleaned, others used as a canvas for the artist to paint directly on to. The whole block feels like a giant atelier: the flats above, belonging to a musician, a painter and an actor, are connected by a stairwell/exhibition space which acts as an extension to the private gallery.

Exarhia to Aigaleo

ADDRESS corner of Chiou and Metaxa Streets
ENGINEER Yannis Tsopanakis
SIZE 740 square metres
BUS B5, A10, B10, A11, A12, B12, 714, 732, 024
ACCESS none

Kyriakos Krokos 1996

Exarhia to Aigaleo

Kyriakos Krokos 1996

Thivon Avenue multi-use building

In response to the diversity of the client's activities, the ground floor and loft of this building serve as open exhibition spaces, while the first floor is given over to offices, and the owner's private office is situated on the second. The orientation of each space depends entirely on its nature: exhibition spaces are positioned towards the main street, the offices and main entrance towards the quieter side street. To protect working spaces from sunlight and, more importantly, the sounds of the main avenue, the façade is set back from the street at an angle and has very few openings.

The main volume of the building follows the edge of the site and is penetrated at an angle by its central core, which forms a separate volume.

ADDRESS 43 Thivon (at corner of Saggariou), Peristeri
CLIENT V Tsipopoulos & Son
ENGINEER Y Tsangarakis (civil)
SIZE 280 square metres
COST 15 million drachmas
BUS A13, 703 TROLLEY 12
ACCESS exhibition areas only

T Papaioannou, D Issaias, G Papakonstantinou 1985

T Papaioannou, D Issaias, G Papakonstantinou 1985

Exarhia to Aigaleo

Bravo coffee factory

Finding this factory can be quite confusing. For some reason there are two number 100s on Kifisou Avenue: one belonging to the Peristeri area and one to the Aigaleo area. Make sure you go to the latter (get off the trolley at the end of Lenorman Street and take bus number 420 left along Kifisou Avenue). Halfway down the avenue, the numbers change and begin again at number 1, so stay calm.

The architect made extensive use of prefabricated elements and traditional construction methods to allow for the factory's future expansion. It was designed around a three-dimensional grid into which standard elements were incorporated in a horizontal or vertical manner, with the possibility of rearranging the spaces at any time according to need. The same idea was applied to the façade (by using a limited selection of standardised panels) and the plans.

Raw materials and packaging are stored in the basement, while the ground floor is for the handling of raw materials and finished products. On the first floor are the personnel area and offices as well as the machinery for the first stage in the processing of the coffee beans. Certain types of beans undergo a further processing on the second floor, and packaging takes place there too. A typical floor plan was created and applied to all four levels; these were then modified to comply with the demands of the different programmes.

ADDRESS 100 Kifisou Avenue, Aigaleo
CLIENT Bravo
ENGINEERS G Poniros, P Ladonikolas
PREFABRICATION Intecta and PROET
BUS A13, A14, B13, B14 TROLLEY 12 to end of Lenorman then bus 420
ACCESS none

Takis Zenetos

Takis Zenetos

Aspropyrgos

Chocotime offices

The strikingly modernist and colourful façade of these chocolate factory offices brings to mind Arquitectonica. The basic frame of the building, two concrete floor slabs on an orthogonal grid of concrete columns, was the starting point.

The two-storey concrete box is pierced by volumes of different colour and shape to disclose the building's new programme and act as a reference to the distinctive and colourful nature of the product. Consequently, the entrance is seen as an ochre sugar cube and the peach-coloured low side wall as a ribbon. A distorted view of a pylon can be glimpsed in the blue glass of the stairwell, which conceals a circular conference room and the adjoining director's office.

The playful nature of the building is accentuated by the freely undulating elements which puncture its surface and reflect fragments of the surrounding environment.

ADDRESS Vrago (industrial district)
CLIENT Chocotime
ASSOCIATE ARCHITECT D Skouroyiannis
SIZE 150 square metres
COST 15 million drachmas
BUS 805
ACCESS by appointment only

Aspropyrgos

Elias Constantopoulos 1991

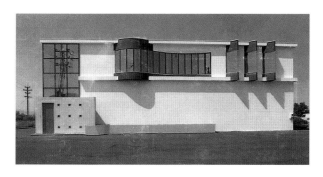

Aspropyrgos

Elias Constantopoulos 1991

Piraeus

Passenger terminal

To appreciate the dynamics of the prestressed-concrete, curved-roof slab of the terminal, drive along the winding coastal road towards Piraeus. As it is positioned diagonally to the road, most of its sides can be seen. The passenger terminal is the most powerful building in Piraeus and one of the most significant modernist buildings in Attica. Awarded first prize in the 1962 competition, it was part of a development study for the whole of the port area, one of whose aims was to resolve the severe traffic jams between the train station and St Nicholas pier.

Two passenger terminals were built at St Nicholas and King Constantine piers to serve ocean liners, as well as a multi-storey port authorities office building on the Karaiskakis coast and a customs office building. Cargo is handled on the ground floor of the terminal, thus restricting the circulation of passengers to the upper two levels. The first floor contains the customs hall, waiting rooms, bars, tourist offices and shops, while the second accommodates the departure lounge, restaurant and bar.

Reinforced concrete was used for both slabs, each spanning 13.5 metres with cantilevers of 6.75 metres. The building rests on columns 1.1 metres in diameter, driven to a depth of 10 metres. The roof slab is carried by frames spanning 22.5 metres, with cantilevers of 8 metres towards the sea and 20.5 metres inland. The larger cantilever is suspended using cables from a frame column rising above the roof. The significant horizontal stress on the column was minimised by using prestressed cables anchored to the second column frame at roof level.

ADDRESS Aghios Nikolaos Pier, Piraeus
CLIENT OLP
ENGINEERS D N Koronaios, G Christou and P Ioannides
BUS 040 (green) TRAIN to Piraeus ACCESS open

J Liapis and I Skroubelos 1969

Piraeus

J Liapis and I Skroubelos 1969

Cafeteria and outdoor swimming pool

The roof of this complex structure brings to mind Spanish urban parks, only this one was not meant to be walked on. Unfortunately the building is now difficult to appreciate as it is in a poor state, but the old photograph on display helps.

The architects treated the roof as the building's fifth elevation, and the way one approaches the scheme becomes part of this unintentional game. The different height levels offer an opportunity to explore the complex in diverse ways and enjoy a variety of views. On the pavement side, a synthesis of concrete and pebble-roof areas address the sea and the city, together with the playful light-well forms that complete the roof's composition. A small narrowing staircase and, to the side, a man-made garden that reflects the composition above, lead you to the entrance, which incorporates a view of the ancient Themistocles wall.

The outdoor swimming pool is no longer in use.

ADDRESS Marina Zeas, Piraeus
CLIENT EOT (Greek Tourist Board)
COLLABORATING ARCHITECT George Makris
TRAIN to Piraeus
ACCESS open

Piraeus

Tasos Biris and Dimitris Biris 1972

Tasos Biris and Dimitris Biris 1972

Mavrakakis office building

The building's positioning, together with the careful arrangement and narrowness of the spaces, ensures efficient cross-ventilation and the best lighting conditions. A metal structure, suspended 67 centimetres in front of the south-east façade of the building, has built-in sunshields and perforated balconies for the window cleaners.

The distinct sloping roof, stainless-steel cavities and triangular metal balconies add to the building's unique character, making it a landmark in the neighbourhood.

ADDRESS Charilaou Trikoupi and Leosthenous Streets, Piraeus
CLIENT John Mavrakakis
COLLABORATING ARCHITECT V Pasiourtides
ENGINEERS A Athanasiades (civil), G Kafetzopoulos (mechanical)
COST 300 million drachmas
SIZE 1000 square metres
BUS 040 (green) TRAIN to Piraeus
ACCESS limited

Piraeus

Atelier 66 (D and S Antonakaki) 1994

Atelier 66 (D and S Antonakaki) 1994

Glyfada, Vouliagmeni

House in Vouliagmeni

Partly submerged in rock, this must be one of the most elegant modernist houses in Athens. The mood was set by linking what appears to be an isolated element – the lift tower – to the house via a covered walkway that breaks through the curved wall to create a dramatic entrance. Both the playfulness of the multi-level arrangement of the spaces and the careful choice of materials take advantage of the site's height differences and best views.

The study, kitchen and living room are on one floor, with the bedrooms isolated on the level above. Lower down and visually connected with the swimming pool is the playroom, an area devoted entirely to the family's leisure activities.

The notion of relaxing, of passing through different levels and enjoying the views, was carried through by using materials similar to those used on yachts, emphasising the poetry of dreams and travelling.

ADDRESS Amalthias Street, Vouliagmeni
INTERIOR ARCHITECT Margerete Janich
BUS 114, 115, 116
ACCESS none

Glyfada, Vouliagmeni

A Van Gilder, B Ioannou, T Sotiropoulos 1993

A Van Gilder, B Ioannou, T Sotiropoulos 1993

Armando Moustaki

This must be one of the most glamorous shops in Glyfada (though it was due to be taken over at the time this guide was being written), specially designed to attract those customers who have seen it all before: American tourists. The brief called for an original dynamic façade to break through all the clichés of display and sweep customers off their feet, leading them into a magical world of childhood dreams and hidden treasures.

A polystyrene, lightly decorated female figure by Stavros Bonatsos revolves slowly inside a glazed, metal-framed tube, reminiscent of the dancing ballerina surrounded by mirrors in an old music box. The theme of time captured by the music box is extended throughout the shop by Panayiotopoulos' series of carefully arranged silk screens. Once over this excitement, customers can concentrate on the shop's equally beautiful merchandise.

ADDRESS 9 Dousmani Street, Glyfada
CLIENT Armando Moustaki
SIZE 35 square metres
COST 14 million drachmas
BUS A3, B3
ACCESS open

George Triantafyllou & Associates 1990

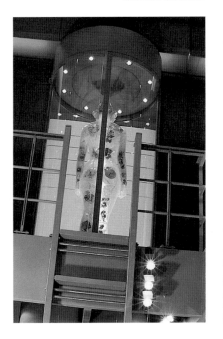

George Triantafyllou & Associates 1990

Aexoni Theatre

The Aexoni Theatre was financed by the Ministry of Environment in 1983 as part of its campaign to restore old quarries. A 'landscape within a landscape' was the concept for this 40-metre-long, 10-metre-high and 7-metre-deep rock sculpture.

To achieve a landscape feel, the sculptor Golanda made use of differently processed volumes referring to flowing water marks and mosaic marble formations reminiscent of concentrations of plant fossils.

Huge volumes of rock were constructed and raised up into tiers of seating, developed to encourage spectators to feel part of the event in progress and of the venue itself.

In September 1992 the theatre staged the 'Art Celebrations of the Aexoni Theatre', devoted to the musician Yannis Xenakis. The use of flowing water on the rocks, combined with Xenakis' contemporary music and light show, opened up a world of possibilities for this impressive installation.

Glyfada, Vouliagmeni

ADDRESS 11 Hydras Street, Aexoni, Glyfada
CLIENT Municipality of Glyfada
SIZE 2.5 hectares
BUS A3, B3 to Glyfada and 128 to Aexoni
ACCESS open; for information telephone 8947 310 or 9680 390-1

Nella Golanda 1985

Nella Golanda 1985

House in Voula

This large structure was designed to house three generations of the same family: parents, children and grandchildren. 'Harmonious co-existence' was the focus of the architects' design.

Two simple geometrical shapes form an interior semi-enclosed space (a parallelogram), interrupted by the existing vegetation, around which the interior spaces are arranged on various levels. The spiralling movement created by this spatial arrangement connects the different levels of the house, with interior and exterior spaces interlocking and overlapping while preserving their own identities. The intentional juxtaposition of the complexity and dynamism of the interior and the static, simplistic nature of the exterior reinforces the architects' original concept.

Glyfada, Vouliagmeni

ADDRESS 11 Valaoritou Street, Voula
ENGINEERS Stelios Papadopoulos and Spyros Malides
CONTRACTOR Takis Deligiorgis
SIZE 500 square metres
BUS A2, 115, 149, 162, 163
ACCESS none

Angelos Altsitzoglou and Yannis Koukis 1993

Angelos Altsitzoglou and Yannis Koukis 1993

Nafsika Astir Palace Hotel

Set in the lee of a cliff on the northern coast of the Mikro Kavouri peninsula, the hotel uses the changing levels of the slope to its advantage. The principal design objective was to integrate the hotel with its natural setting and transform a spoilt beach into a garden resort. On the south side, the building's height was kept lower than the hill so that it would not block the wooded ridge. The trees are protected from the sea by a breakwater.

The main characteristics of the building are its vertical and horizontal terraced arrangement and the relationship between communal and private spaces. In a reversal of the usual arrangement, communal areas occupy the upper levels, while the snack bar, changing rooms and a number of semi-independent guest rooms with private gardens are placed at ground level by the sea. The four intermediate levels contain spacious rooms and suites, each with a private balcony.

All exterior surfaces are of exposed light-grey concrete with sliding aluminium-framed French windows. The floors of the reception areas are covered in dark-grey marble; some of the walls feature works in bas-relief and murals by the artists Paris Prekas and Michalis Kantzourakis.

The hotel is based on the prize-winning design submitted by the three architects in a 1973 architectural competition.

ADDRESS Mikro Kavouri Peninsula, Vouliagmeni
ENGINEERS H Teleionis and G Theodosiou, A Basakos
LANDSCAPE DESIGN I Hitzanidou-Vlahaki
BUS A3 to Glyfada and 114 to Kavouri
ACCESS open

Glyfada, Vouliagmeni

E Vourekas, A Georgiades and C Dekavallas 1979

Glyfada, Vouliagmeni

E Vourekas, A Georgiades and C Dekavallas 1979

Villa in Kavouri

The villa, used as a permanent residence, is located on the peninsula of Kavouri. It consists of two levels: the upper one contains the main reception areas, master bedroom and service spaces, and the lower one the children's rooms and staff quarters, storage rooms, heating plant and sauna. The villa is constructed mainly with reinforced-concrete slabs and steel columns; exterior masonry walls are painted white, with sliding French windows and shutters in varnished wood. All levels have terracotta tiles and floor-to-ceiling soundproof panels serving as partitions and sliding doors. Some of the interior wall surfaces are covered with hand-made ceramic tiles by Elena Vernadaki, based on designs by the well-known Greek painter Yannis Moralis.

The architect's main objective was to integrate the house with its environment, taking advantage of natural light and ventilation. Acrylic dome structures on the roof capture the winter light and redirect it to the centre of the house. During the summer these domes are covered, but can be opened for ventilation. The roof, which is covered in white marble chips, provides an additional form of insulation: a layer of water deflects the sun's rays and cools the house down while the water evaporates.

Glyfada, Vouliagmeni

ADDRESS Kavouri, Vouliagmeni
BUS A3 to Glyfada and 114 to Kavouri
ACCESS none

Constantin Dekavallas 1971

Glyfada, Vouliagmeni

Constantin Dekavallas 1971

Saronida, Sounio, Markopoulo

Vacation home in Saronida

Despite many restrictions, this holiday home is a very elegant addition to the bold landscape that surrounds it. The architect has sensitively arranged the spaces so that the view continues to unfold as you move around the house.

The careful arrangement of spaces was prompted by the desire to keep the house on one level so it could follow the garden, although this was not eventually possible because of the site's 45-degree slope. This difficulty was resolved by making small changes in level so that on travelling through the house you effectively change floors.

The building was designed using the minimum amount of construction details, and with traditional materials and techniques to avoid any supervision difficulties with the local builders. A turned-over tiled roof was designed specially for the collection of rain water, which is then redirected and stored in an underground water tank for everyday housework.

ADDRESS Saronida, Sounio
CLIENT Delotis
COST 30 million drachmas
SIZE 120 square metres
BUS Athens–Sounio bus from Pedio Areos (40 minutes to Saronida on the way to Sounio; 10-minute walk from the bus stop)
ACCESS none

K Kontozoglou

Saronida, Sounio, Markopoulo

K Kontozoglou

Lanaras residence, Anavyssos

Based on modernist prototypes of the 1960s and built on a large site on top of a hill, this family summer house stands out from all the others on the coast. The architect's aim was to create an unobstructed view of the Saronic Gulf with the use of a glazed volume and sliding openings along the entire length of the façade, contained within two slabs. The two parallel concrete slabs span from the main living area towards the sea and are supported only by thin steel columns, creating a feeling of freedom and escapism. An architect, inspired by the house, once wrote: '... The ceiling looks like a starry sky, the dining table appears to float over the sea.' A truly ideal holiday home.

Saronida, Sounio, Markopoulo

ADDRESS Sounio Avenue, Anavyssos, Saronida (47 kilometres from Athens)
CLIENT Lanaras
CIVIL ENGINEER Nahnikian
SIZE 600 square metres
BUS Athens–Sounio bus from Pedio Areos
ACCESS none

Nicos Valsamakis 1963

Nicos Valsamakis 1963

Paraschis residence, Anavyssos

Very close to the Lanaras residence (see previous entry) and built along the same principles, this house (also by Valsamakis) is as not as daring as its neighbour. Apparently the clients' fear of long cantilevers contained the architect's desire for spans reaching well out to sea. Instead, the lower plane, with beams like teeth, seems to be clinging on to the edge.

The plan is organised on a grid and on three planes which more or less define the dimensions and the functional units of the residence: the living area extends towards the sea while the kitchen and the bedrooms overlook opposite aspects of the landscape.

Saronida, Sounio, Markopoulo

ADDRESS Sounio Avenue, Anavyssos, Saronida (47 kilometres from Athens)
CLIENT Paraschis
ENGINEER Nahnikian
SIZE 300 square metres
BUS Athens–Sounio bus from Pedio Areos
ACCESS none

Nicos Valsamakis 1963

Nicos Valsamakis 1963

House in Legrena

This house, situated on the coastal road between Athens and Sounio, is on a small hill by the sea, at Legrena village near the ancient temple of Poseidon. Three walls create the basis for its composition. Two parallel stone walls define the entrance and the living room, emphasising the view to the sea; vertical to them, a freestanding wall with uniform repetitive openings defines and transforms the outdoor spaces.

Adjoining these walls are three separate volumes: the kitchen, the children's two-level bedrooms and the parents' bedroom (part of the original building). The arrangement of the walls and volumes creates outdoor rooms with different views and orientations.

A transverse view – from the land to the sea and the temple of Poseidon – is achieved by the two glass partitions that form the entrance. Although these may mark the limits of the structure, the stunning view transports the viewer across the sea to the horizon and beyond.

Saronida, Sounio, Markopoulo

ADDRESS Sounio Avenue, Legrena, Sounio
(56 kilometres from Athens)
ENGINEERS G Hadgistergiou and H Argyros
SIZE 250 square metres
COST 50 million drachmas
BUS Athens–Sounio bus from Pedio Areos
ACCESS none

M Kokkinou, A Kourkoulas 1990

Saronida, Sounio, Markopoulo

M Kokkinou, A Kourkoulas 1990

Apartment block

Built on one of the highest points of Markopoulo, this two-storey block has three large and two smaller apartments. The structure was given a simple and austere look so as to counteract the chaos created by the other buildings that surround it.

Although site restrictions dictated two separate buildings (resting on columns and following the slope of the land), the architects have achieved a cohesive feel by using the stairwell in two ways: physically, it provides access to both buildings and, socially, it brings them together by providing semi-enclosed common-use areas.

Saronida, Sounio, Markopoulo

ADDRESS Georgiou Pini Street
CLIENT Daremas family
ENGINEER M Spyridakis
SIZE 600 square metres
COST 25 million drachmas
BUS from Pedio Areos take the bus to Markopoulo
ACCESS none

Spyros Rogan, John Papasideris 1981

Spyros Rogan, John Papasideris 1981

Filothei, P. Psychiko

House in Filothei

This house, characteristic of Krokos' style, is situated right next to the Filothei stream, the main topographical influence on the organisation of spaces and, inevitably, the exterior. It consists of four levels: basement, ground floor, first floor and roof.

The basement, apart from the usual utility areas, contains a multi-use 'secret' room, lit by glass bricks from the south side of the ground floor and from certain points where the ground level has been lowered. The ground level, which is raised one metre above street level, develops over two levels (with a height difference of half a metre) which contain the entrance, hall, kitchen and working area. From the first-floor bedrooms one can take the lift or stairs to the small guest house on the roof or sit in the roof's outdoor living spaces.

The house was designed to reveal its reinforced-concrete structure and cement-block walls. For the architect it was a chance to rediscover the art of building and to explore the potential of the materials and their relationship in terms of colour and tone.

Filothei, P. Psychiko

ADDRESS 6 Zosima Street, Filothei
ENGINEERS Yannis Tsopanakis and Yerasimos Maratos
SIZE 543 square metres
BUS 610
ACCESS none

Kyriakos Krokos 1991

Kyriakos Krokos 1991

Valsamakis residence

To avoid disappointment, contact the owner to make an appointment to visit this house – its beauty cannot be appreciated just by walking past its mysterious wooden façade.

Set in an affluent suburb of Athens on a small site, the house is basically a one-level, walk-through rectangle with large, wooden, sliding openings on to the patio and swimming pool. The one large living space is sub-divided by three walls which define functional zones and secondary spaces.

This is a 'hi-tech' house, especially by Greek standards, in which detailed constructions are subjected to the discipline of a grid and services incorporated within a thin, reinforced-concrete slab resting on slim metal supports and wooden internal partitions. All materials are left in their natural state with neither paint nor rendering.

A very simple but glamorous house.

ADDRESS 22 Niovis Street, Filothei
CLIENT Nicos Valsamakis
CIVIL ENGINEER S Angelides
MECHANICAL ENGINEER A Angelides
SIZE 170 square metres
BUS 610
ACCESS by arrangement with owner

Filothei, P. Psychiko

Nicos Valsamakis 1963

Filothei, P. Psychiko

Nicos Valsamakis 1963

Kavvadas residence

This house, one of the largest designed by Valsamakis, sits on a suburban hill overlooking the city. Its skyline figure and massive masonry structure relate to the slope of the street. When one enters the house, because of the positioning of the reception and living areas, a direct view of Athens is at once revealed. The lower level makes use of the inclination of the ground to accommodate bedrooms, the covered swimming pool and the auxiliary spaces.

With its white, rough-plastered surfaces and timber lofts, the scheme breaks away from older 1960s modernist projects.

Filothei, P. Psychiko

ADDRESS Markou Botsari and Athanasiou Diakou, Filothei
CLIENT N Kavvadas
ENGINEER N Kavvadas
BUS A7, 550, 610
ACCESS none

Nicos Valsamakis 1974

Filothei, P. Psychiko

Nicos Valsamakis 1974

Alexakis two-family house

The design of this house – in Psychiko, a suburb of Athens – is based around a large rectangular prism that constitutes the core of the building, carefully positioned on site to form courtyards for the two residences. The ground floor, a single-level residence for a small family, has two bedrooms facing the courtyards on either side of the building. The much larger upper residence is developed over four levels and has three bedrooms and a guest house right at the top.

Privacy for both dwellings is achieved by positioning the entrances on different sides of the prism. The corridor-like core grows and extends vertically and horizontally to accommodate the activities on either side of it, both forming and uniting the two separate residences.

Filothei, P. Psychiko

ADDRESS Solomou and Souri Streets, Paleo Psychiko
CLIENT Alexakis
COLLABORATING ARCHITECT Aleka Monemvasitou
ENGINEER V Plaenis
BUS 603
ACCESS by arrangement with owners

Atelier 66 (D and S Antonakaki) 1982

Filothei, P. Psychiko

Atelier 66 (D and S Antonakaki) 1982

Karakosta residence

For her own residence, Seva Karakosta made good use of demolition materials and elements to create an uncomplicated design in which simple everyday life could be enjoyed. The house is orientated to take advantage of the best lighting conditions and views, and its structure and materials are exposed, emphasising the simple and natural feel. Three basic colours (red, yellow and blue) are used to bring out certain architectural elements and at the same time make references to the Greek islands and the Greek vernacular tradition.

The house, one of the architect's first projects, was also one of the most important for it was used as a vehicle for Karakosta to express herself in a new abstract manner, free from the decorative mannerisms in vogue at the time. Thirty years on, it is still considered a modern house.

Filothei, P. Psychiko

ADDRESS 74 Diamantidou Street, Paleo Psychiko
ENGINEER I Pomonis
SIZE 180 square metres
COST 350,000 drachmas
BUS A7
TROLLEY 13
ACCESS limited (consult owner)

Seva Karakosta 1967

Seva Karakosta 1967

House in Aghia Paraskevi

This house in a middle-class suburb of Athens, on a small almost shoe-shaped site, was designed by a young, enthusiastic architect eager to test his knowledge and influences in a Greek context. His love for classical architecture, especially eighteenth-century French buildings and Palladio's villas and palaces, is apparent in the organisation and use of space in this very modern house.

The living room, hall and dining room are positioned on an axis forming a 14-metre-long uniform space – an arrangement using repeated doors and openings, as found in classical architecture. All spaces – apart from the kitchen and bathrooms – are designed for a variety of uses, making references to the diagrammatic, non-functionalist arrangement of spaces in classical architecture and also catering for the residents' changing needs. The house's diagonal position on site makes maximum use of daylight penetration into its enclosed and semi-enclosed spaces, creating a continuous movement throughout the day.

On the back of the house, the nursery – a three-storey-high, round pergola resembling a castle – was designed to stimulate the children's imagination. The architect felt that with its variety of forms, heights, sizes and colours, 'this house would seem like a city in relation to the children and their sense of scale'.

ADDRESS 13 Saki Karagiorga Street, Aghia Paraskevi
CLIENTS Antonis and Helen Papadopoulou
ENGINEERS T Christou and K Plingerakos
SIZE 217 square metres and 140 square metres (basement)
COST 50 million drachmas
BUS A5, 406
ACCESS none

Filothei, P. Psychiko

George Panetsos 1992

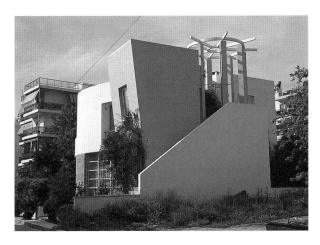

Filothei, P. Psychiko

George Panetsos 1992

Halandri, Polydroso, Marousi

Tsalas residence

This three-level building, resting on a corner site, is in fact the architect's permanent residence. The shape of the south-facing site, together with a 4-metre-wide flowerbed, encouraged the design of an elongated structure with large openings. The same language was carried through to the interior where a triangular opening in the floor of the first level forms a double volume with the ground level, accentuated by the penetrating light that visually unifies them. A reflection of this gesture is noted on the ground level, directly under the opening, in the form of a triangular recess in the floor, filled with pebbles.

The architect's design principle was to create an energy-efficient house to minimise heat loss. The reinforced-concrete walls were carefully damp-proofed and insulated from the inside and all openings protected with roller shutters and awnings. Because the north side of the ground floor and basement is below ground level (due to the site's sudden change in height), heat losses are further minimised.

The area surrounding this residence has been pedestrianised and turned into a passage leading towards a large piece of land that includes the Halandri gorge, one of the city's few recreation centres.

Halandri, Polydroso, Marousi

ADDRESS 31 A Diakou and M Botsari, Halandri
CLIENT Christos Tsalas
ENGINEERS Michael Pittas, Nikos Bartsakoulias and Stavros Dimitriou
SIZE 270 square metres
COST 45 million drachmas
BUS 402, 450
ACCESS none

Christos Tsalas 1996

Halandri, Polydroso, Marousi

Christos Tsalas 1996

Halandri apartment block

Five individual dwellings, capturing the character of the Halandri suburb, make up this modernist housing complex. Although the scheme was subject to the financial constraints of the part-exchange building method (*antiparohi*) it is not a typical housing block with a standardised unit repeated on every floor. Each apartment occupies two floors, with the separated living and sleeping spaces visually connected by the use of a double volume.

A parapet running the entire length of the façade brings all the dwellings together and forms outdoor, enclosed or semi-enclosed spaces.

Halandri, Polydroso, Marousi

ADDRESS Zan Moreas and Spetson Streets, Halandri
ENGINEER John Demopoulos
SIZE 654 square metres
COST 100 million drachmas, including the garden
BUS 421, 441, 450
ACCESS none

Karerina Vasilarou 1995

Halandri, Polydroso, Marousi

Karerina Vasilarou 1995

Papanikoli Street office building

Most avenues in Athens are lined with endless rows of characterless glazed monsters imposing their presence with their tackiness and enormity and pretending to be the ultimate in high-tech design. Helen and George Manetas came to the rescue and proved that it is possible to design a large-scale, glazed building without necessarily compromising aesthetic values. This office building is an example of what can be achieved with a few simple elements and a modicum of sensitivity.

A white concrete frame (a change from the 'fashionable' apricot colour) grows out of the building's glazed façade, giving it a sense of scale and an indication of where the floors might be. This simple element – and others such as the metal staircase and the ledge running along the façade addressing the street – breaks up the monotony and brings a sense of lightness to the building.

Very refreshing when compared with your average 'glass box'.

Halandri, Polydroso, Marousi

ADDRESS Papanikoli Street, Halandri
ENGINEER C Telionis
CONTRACTOR P Karayiannis
SIZE 1800 square metres
COST 500 million drachmas
BUS A7, 421, 441
ACCESS limited

Helen and George Manetas 1991

Halandri, Polydroso, Marousi

Helen and George Manetas 1991

Polydroso apartment block

This apartment block was designed around the concept of a vertical neighbourhood. It comprises six one-level flats and nine two-level, maisonette-type flats. Unlike the commercial apartment blocks in Athens in which most of the flats look towards the same view, these apartments have been designed to frame specific views and to relate to the surrounding flats as if in a neighbourhood. Note the arrangement of the balconies: they are of various sizes, with some extending outwards or positioned diagonally; one is never directly above another, blocking its light.

The opening up of the apartment block towards itself encourages a certain way of life and behaviour between the residents, adding an extra layer to the meaning of symbiosis.

ADDRESS 22 Chrysanthemon Street, Polydroso
BUS 402, 449, 450, 550
ACCESS none

T Biris, D Biris, M Kafritsa

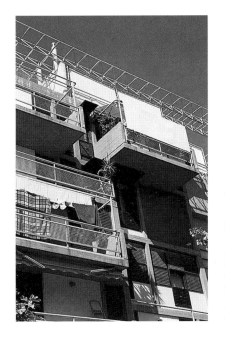

Halandri, Polydroso, Marousi

T Biris, D Biris, M Kafritsa

Polydroso office complex

The office buildings for three individual companies have been incorporated into one large complex. The surrounding landscape appears mature, as existing olive trees have been left and others transplanted. The environment is enhanced by a pond, a sculpture designed by Yorgos Zogolopoulos and the wooden decks that lead to buildings B and C.

All the buildings are clad with fair-faced cement bricks which, combined with the exterior insulation, provide ventilation for the façade. Building A, the offices of TEB SA (a well-known contracting company in Greece), houses mechanical installations under its double-pitched steel roof, providing cross-ventilation and shading to the roof below. Building B shelters two engineering companies while Building C (with approximately 1000 square metres for 60 people) contains the architects' own offices.

The aim of the design was to provide the best possible working environment by controlling the light, sound and temperature of the virtually open three-level space. Daylight is bounced off suspended white fabric reflectors to the lower levels and apertures are shaded with motor-operated vertical fabric blinds to control glare (particularly important where computers are in use). The ideal temperature is preserved by a combination of cross-ventilation, ceiling fans, roof extraction fans and an air-conditioning system that automatically switches on when the temperature exceeds 29 degrees centigrade. Cooling is further assisted by two extractor fans on the roof which operate only when the temperature reaches a certain level.

Because of the large open interior, special attention was paid to acoustics. Metal panels, suspended from the concrete decks of the different levels, allow for the movement of air between the panels and the ceilings, balancing out the sound. Even the wooden treads of the stairs are specially

Halandri, Polydroso, Marousi

Meletitiki – A N Tombazis and Associates Architects Ltd 1990–95

fixed to the steel support beams to eliminate the transfer of vibration from the tread to the frame.

The creation of a controlled environment and the attention to detail are technically impressive, particularly for Greece, but one is left wondering whether such technically controlled environments are appropriate in the Greek climate – or beneficial for their occupants.

ADDRESS 25–7 Monemvasias and Akakion Streets, Polydroso
OWNERS TEB SA (building A), Dromos AEM and Epsilon International SA (building B), A and A Tombazis (building C)
ASSOCIATED ARCHITECTS A Demetiou, S Paraskevopoulou, Y Romanos
CIVIL ENGINEERS T Tsimonos (building A), I Mylonas, S Tzivilakis (buildings B and C)
M&E LDK Consultants, Engineers and Planners Ltd, D Kirimilidis (project engineer)
STRUCTURAL ENGINEER OMETE SA (C Kostikas, project engineer, G Iacovidis and P Kremezis, consulting engineers)
ENERGY CONSULTANT The National and Kapodistrian University of Athens, Environmental Studies (Professor M Santamouris)
ACOUSTICS Dr G Schubert
CONTRACTOR TEB SA (for building A; co-ordinators for buildings B and C)
SIZE 1922 square metres (building A), 986 square metres (building B), 1027 square metres (building C)
BUS A7, 402, 550
ACCESS none

Meletitiki – A N Tombazis and Associates Architects Ltd 1990–95

Meletitiki – A N Tombazis and Associates Architects Ltd 1990–95

Atrina office building

Because planning regulations no longer allow such tall buildings, there are only two tower blocks in Athens. Both were designed by Vikelas, but under different political regimes. The first one, the Athens tower on Vasilissis Sofias Avenue, was built in 1969 during the colonels' dictatorship; the second, Atrina, in 1980 after democracy had been restored.

Both are similar in plan, with the stairwells, lifts and toilets placed in the centre creating a service core, and the offices and conference halls placed around the edge. The Atrina tower makes a subtle attempt to break away from the rigidity of the rectangular plan by breaking into three interconnecting parts while still reading as a whole. The height difference between these three sections provides a sense of scale.

Halandri, Polydroso, Marousi

ADDRESS Kifissias Avenue, Paradisos Amarousiou
BUS A7, 550
ACCESS none

J Vikelas 1980

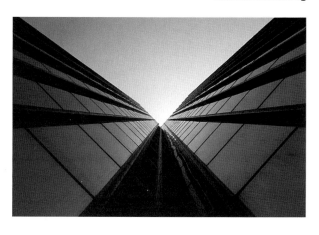

Halandri, Polydroso, Marousi

J Vikelas 1980

Offices for Mechaniki and Generali

This award-winning scheme for three office buildings and two underground car parks is on a 2.5-hectare corner site just off the busy Kifissias Avenue on the way to Marousi. The architects saw the potential of the site's position – against the existing city grid that runs parallel to Kifissias – and have exploited it to the max. And it was this opposition to the grid that set the mood of the project.

A 14- by 100-metre slab with a parallel access road emphasises the site's diagonal placing. Two buildings, essentially a triangle and a 21-metre-square cube on either side of the rectangular slab, are further elements in this game of geometry. The playfulness of these shapes is accentuated by the use of colour: rusty brown for the five-floor slab (the headquarters of the Generali insurance company), yellow ochre for the seven-level cube, grey for the five-storey triangle (both owned by Mechaniki). All materials and methods of construction are of a standard not found too often in Greece.

Halandri, Polydroso, Marousi

ADDRESS M Alexandrou and V Sofias Streets, Marousi
CONSULTANT ARCHITECT Ioannis Peponis
ASSOCIATE ARCHITECTS Louiza Yannousi, Ioannis Ditsas, Iro Bertaki, Elli Leptourgou, Kostas Panigiris, Antonia Panou
ENGINEERS F Karydakis, T Kamarinos
CONTRACTOR Mechaniki
SIZE 8000 square metres
COST 2 billion drachmas
BUS A7, 550
ACCESS limited

M Kokkinou, A Kourkoulas 1996

Halandri, Polydroso, Marousi

M Kokkinou, A Kourkoulas 1996

Private exhibition space and residence

The brief called for a private exhibition space and residence as well as a sculpture park on a 24-hectare sloping site, where an old stone mansion destroyed by fire was to be preserved as a ruin.

The site and the client's requirements led to the positioning of small structures along a man-made horizontal plane. A 200-metre-long strip which forms the spine of the otherwise scattered design is counter-balanced by the rigidity and simplicity of the independent structures through the use of common basic materials (concrete, wood, stone and aluminium).

The sides of the building parallel to the retaining wall have no openings, whereas the others are completely transparent with views towards Penteli mountain and the city. This transverse transparency, which follows the main movement through the building, creates interpenetrating volumes and changes in scale, emphasised by the different sized openings and construction details. The glazed surfaces can be blocked off with white Venetian blinds or wooden roller shutters, creating a game of ever-changing façades.

ADDRESS at the end of Finikon Street, Anavryta, Marousi
CLIENT Prodromos and Helen Emfietzoglou
COLLABORATING ARCHITECT Christos Papoulias (phase A)
CONSULTING ARCHITECTS George Minotos, Dominiki Minotou, Kate Alexandropoulou
ENGINEERS Nikos Avgerinos, George Hatzopoulos
LANDSCAPING Arboretum Agricultural
SIZE 3500 square metres
BUS A7, 550
ACCESS art gallery and sculpture park open to the public

Catherine Diakomides, Nikos Haritos 1996

Halandri, Polydroso, Marousi

Catherine Diakomides, Nikos Haritos 1996

Manetas office and residence

A metal structure is such a rare sight in this concrete city, especially in a residential neighbourhood.

The house was designed and built in two phases, transforming over the years in response to the architects/clients' developing needs, taking into account the changes in their lives and way of thinking. The first part was designed to accommodate two houses – one for the architects themselves (with a loft) and one for their parents – using the style and techniques formed during their studies: double volumes, round columns, structural walls and so on. After a few years the loft was turned into a bedroom, a bigger kitchen was added, then a studio and, finally, in 1991, the office. The metal structure of the latter, chosen for its lightness and versatility, gave the architects the opportunity to experiment and explore the potential of this material to the full. The results are impressive.

Halandri, Polydroso, Marousi

ADDRESS 19 Mytilenes and 22 Kountourioti Streets, Marousi
SIZE 90 square metres (office), 300 square metres (1968 building)
COST 20 million drachmas (office), 1.5 million drachmas (1968 building)
BUS A7, 41, 550
ACCESS limited

Helen and George Manetas 1968 and 1991

Halandri, Polydroso, Marousi

Helen and George Manetas 1968 and 1991

Neo Herakleio, Pefki

House in Neo Herakleio

In the northern suburbs of Athens, this elegant, contemporary, two-storey family house fronts a narrow busy street and sits on a very tight site, rubbing shoulders with an apartment block to the right and the parents' home to the left.

Since it was important for the extended family to eat together around an outdoor oven in the garden, the house was located to the right of the site, allowing the space between the parents' home and the new house to develop as a gathering place. As a result, the right side has no openings and folds into an inverted L, creating a space between the entrance bridge and the main staircase. The opposite side has windows, a door and a chimney similar to those on the facing side of the parents' home.

With these two sides determined by the narrowness of the site and the dictates of building regulations, the new house sits on a north–south axis between the quiet, dark, back garden and the noisy, sunny street. Thus, the other two sides, more sections than elevations, become expressions of the landscape's passage through the house.

The house unfolds vertically on three levels. The middle level, where the entrance bridge penetrates the two-storey glazing, is seen as an intermediate stage in a continuous labyrinthine movement that organises the levels of the house.

The layout of a Greek courtyard, where one enters from one side and crosses diagonally to the door, was the inspiration for the entrance. The same principle appears in elevation: one enters on the right and moves diagonally to the left, either up towards the balcony or down towards the sunken court.

Materials and paint are used to emphasise movement and function. Colour defines each volume (blue for the kitchen, red for the bedrooms), articulating the 'façade as section'.

Neo Herakleio, Pefki

Ioannis Zachariades and Athanasios Spanomarides 1994

Neo Herakleio, Pefki

Ioannis Zachariades and Athanasios Spanomarides 1994

The architects insist that these principles 'allow us to get away from the sterile concept of the "outline" – distinctly separating an ordered interior from an ungodly exterior – that is the core of Western architecture. Instead, we base our work on the Greek notion of an open-ended space experienced through movement as a section.'

Neo Herakleio, Pefki

ADDRESS 53 Iroon Polytechneiou Street, Neo Herakleio
CLIENT Mr and Mrs Demetracopoulos
ENGINEERS John Ermopoulos and Athanasios Yiannopoulos
SIZE 240 square metres
COST 40 million drachmas
TRAIN Neo Herakleio, then a five-minute walk
ACCESS limited (consult owners)

Ioannis Zachariades and Athanasios Spanomarides 1994

Ioannis Zachariades and Athanasios Spanomarides 1994

Solar Village 3, Lykovryssi

As the result of an agreement made in 1978 between BMFT of West Germany and the Greek government, the Solar Village Company was created to execute a project in the field of low-temperature solar energy.

A 435-family community was equipped with various solar-energy and energy-conservation systems: nine rows of houses have rooftop air collectors, short-term bedrock storage units and air-distribution systems; 40 units have water collectors and short-term water-storage tanks; 24 apartments use an interstitial water storage system designed around a 500-cubic-metre semi-underground steel storage tank; 34 units have passive solar heating and cooling systems with electricity from the local grid to meet peak demands; 12 apartments use a direct solar-gain system, a greenhouse and Trombe walls; 22 houses have one of six passive solar systems. At the heart of the project are two diesel-fired heat pumps that supply hot water to the radiators of individual houses.

The basic energy-conservation design saves an estimated 65 per cent of conventional energy consumption. With passive solar heating meeting 70 per cent of the remaining annual load, the energy used by the Solar Village housing is about 10 per cent of national average consumption.

ADDRESS 1 Iliou Street, Pefki-Lykovryssi (18 kilometres north of Athens)
OWNER Workers Housing Organisation (OEK)
PROJECT CO-ORDINATOR Solar Village SA (C Kanaris, director)
M&E LDK (L Damianides and D Kirimlides)
ENERGY CONSULTANTS Vivian Loftness-Hartkopf, D Daskalakis
ACTIVE SYSTEMS (design/construction) Interatom GmbH, Germany
CONTRACTOR Mechaniki SA STRUCTURE K Mylonas (civil engineer)
SIZE 25,000 square metres COST 4.5 billion drachmas
BUS A7, 507, 550 ACCESS open

Neo Herakleio, Pefki

A N Tombazis and Associates Architects Ltd 1984–89

Neo Herakleio, Pefki

A N Tombazis and Associates Architects Ltd 1984–89

Marathon to Ekali

House and guest houses in Schinias

The concept for this house is based on the idea of a petrified ship on a shore facing two focal points on the horizon. The need to preserve the dynamics, if not the image, of this initial gesture led to a paring down of the means of expression and the use of details as a vehicle for carrying through and emphasising the idea. The colour scheme was directly related to the landscape: rusty brown, sienna, grey and yellow ochre.

What makes this scheme unique is the later addition of a guest wing based on the design of a monastery courtyard with a chapel in the middle. The chapel is now in full use and has its very own priest. Some changes had to be made to the house, though. Apparently, the sight of the naked male statue on the terrace overlooking the sea was offensive to the Christian community and had to be moved. Otherwise, both schemes fit together and co-exist harmoniously, creating a sense of community despite being designed several years apart.

ADDRESS Settlement for Judges and Attorneys (Oikismos dikaston ke Eisaggeleon), Schinias, Marathon
CLIENT Christos Kerasiotis
SIZE 700 square metres
COST 300 million drachmas
BUS from Pedio Areos to Schinias
ACCESS none

A Manidakis, M Manidakis, H Haritatos 1986–92

A Manidakis, M Manidakis, H Haritatos 1986–92

Marathonas racecourse

This massive project, winner of the Marathonas Racecourse Competition, captures the glory of Ancient Greece and the spirit of the Olympic Games. Besides the racetrack, there are changing rooms, a VIP and press room, a medical centre, a gym, a football ground, open-air basketball and volleyball pitches, offices, parking facilities and seating for 2500 people.

The racecourse is positioned on the site where Spyros Louis won the 42-kilometre Marathon run at the first Olympic Games, held in Athens in 1896 (the reason the Greeks felt they had the right to the Olympiad in 1996). The Marathon is a celebration of Pheidippides' run in 490 BC from Marathon to Athens, where he died after announcing the Greek victory over the Persians in the famous message 'Nenikikamen' (we won). Since it was re-established in the 1960s by Lambrakis, a politician and Marathon runner, this long-distance race symbolising freedom and peace has become a permanent feature of the Olympic Games.

Marathonas racecourse feels like a landscape embossment around the main event. The perspective view formed focuses on the starting point, which is emphasised by a sculpture carved with long straight lines – a reminder to the athletes of the long journey ahead.

ADDRESS Marathonas Avenue, Marathon
STRUCTURAL ENGINEERS OMETE SA and A Athanasiades
MECHANICAL ENGINEERS HM EPE
MODEL PHOTOGRAPHY Charalambos Loizides
SIZE 23.5 hectares
BUS from Pedio Areos to Marathonas
ACCESS open

T Xanthi, Y Zakynthinos with T Androulakis and P Zervos 1996

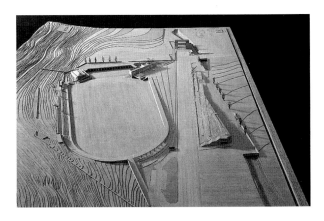

T Xanthi, Y Zakynthinos with T Androulakis and P Zervos 1996

Delta industrial complex

This industrial complex for Delta SA, the largest Greek dairy, constitutes one of the biggest investments of its kind in the country. The project consists mainly of a new yogurt-making facility (comprising an extended office area and the main ice-cream cold store), as well as a large sewage treatment plant.

What Delta had in mind was a unique industrial complex where the architecture would not be dominated by the complicated mechanical substructure that its business demanded. In order to achieve this, the vast production areas and utility spaces are incorporated in a global design, approached both functionally and aesthetically.

The project encompasses all levels of intervention, from the landscaping of the site and the arrangement of the vehicular circulation network to the design of furniture for specific spaces.

ADDRESS Aghios Stefanos (on the Athens–Lamia Highway)
CLIENT Delta SA
STRUCTURAL ENGINEER OMETE SA
M&E Fasma Consulting Engineers Ltd
SIZE 30,000 square metres
COST 15 billion drachmas
BUS 508, 509
ACCESS limited

V Baskozos, N Passaloglou, D Tsangaraki 1994

Würth Hellas industrial complex

The headquarters complex of the German firm Würth is, as the Germans say, the 'Vorsprung durch technik' of Greece. The design was chosen and presented at an international conference on industrial buildings held in Sardinia in May 1989.

The structure consists of three basic units: the office building, the factory building, and the cylindrical connecting element which defines the overall volumetric form. Basically, the architect has designed a shell for this assembly factory – using Alucobond and granite to clad the offices and polyurethane sheets for the industrial parts. At the entrance the specially lit arch, combined with the red column, has become an easily recognisable feature for visitors.

The architect feels that the building is best viewed at night (from a speeding car on the motorway) when its dramatic, almost fragmented, qualities are heightened.

ADDRESS Kryoneri (23 kilometres out of Athens on Athens–Lamia Highway)
CLIENT Würth
ENGINEER T Bobotis
SIZE 4700 square metres
BUS 508, 509
ACCESS limited

T Bobotis 1991

T Bobotis 1991

Voyatzoglou showroom

This showroom occupies two floors, with a clear distinction between the two main ranges of products supplied by the company. On the ground floor, small-scale furniture fittings, accessories, DIY systems and products are displayed. On the first floor are the larger-scale modular systems used in commercial spaces such as supermarkets, retail stores and warehouses.

For the ground-floor showroom, a flexible display system for the ever-changing range of products has been devised using a variety of interlinked spaces. In order to counterbalance this fluctuation, the various parts of the showroom are visually and spatially unified by a curved timber wall pierced by small glass openings and display cases. This element also helps to separate the display area from the personnel offices and to direct movement from the front to the back of the building.

On the first floor, the large-scale modular systems determined most of the spatial arrangements. Intervention was thus limited to the entrance and exit spaces, particularly the transitional area between the standardised and the more sophisticated, individualised systems. The glass door separating these two spaces is sand-blasted and features the profiles and shapes of elements used in the products exhibited.

Wire-frame trolleys are stored in the entrance space, where their shadows on the walls create an impressive and dramatic effect.

ADDRESS 12 kilometres out of Athens on Athens–Lamia Highway
CLIENT Voyatzoglou
COLLABORATOR Nicos Constantopoulos
ASSOCIATE DESIGNER D Skouroyiannis
SIZE 1000 square metres
COST 15 million drachmas
ACCESS open

Marathon to Ekali

Elias Constantopoulos 1995

Elias Constantopoulos 1995

Stamata solar house

Based on the design of the very first solar house (belonging to Socrates!), this passive solar house is set at the back of a 5-hectare site enjoying the southern view and the front garden. The brief called for a family house and an independent 30-square-metre guest house.

The structure was broken down into volumes and spread over many levels, following the slope of the site and the course of the sun. Four existing pine trees now stand between two of the three volumes and have become a feature, together with the glazed stairwell that provides a visual and physical connection between house and garden. The three main volumes are arranged around a courtyard which opens up towards the street and the west garden and acts as an everyday living space.

The interior spaces are arranged over many small changes in level that overall occupy two floors. After entering on the ground floor, through the living room, one is led to a central space with a raised balcony and a dining room overlooking the courtyard, a smaller dining room and the kitchen. The living room gives access both to a lower office level and a higher, master-bedroom level, heated by a Trombe-type wall and equipped with a greenhouse on its balcony. This feature is also found on the balcony of the first-floor living room. A staircase leads up through the children's bedrooms to the terrace, the only flat roof. The others are sloped to take advantage of the sun's movement and other weather conditions.

ADDRESS 5 Profiti Ilia Street, Profitis Ilias, Stamata
CLIENT Constantinos Angelopoulos
CIVIL ENGINEER T Gogos
SIZE 550 square metres
COST 35 million drachmas
BUS A7, 507, 550 ACCESS none

Michael Souvatzidis 1990

Michael Souvatzidis 1990

House in Drosia

The architect has always been fascinated by the way the Japanese handle concrete – with sensitivity and respect, exploring the material's limits and possibilities and creating new ways of using it. As it is a material widely used in the Greek building industry, Kaltsa bravely decided to adopt the Japanese approach and test the possibilities for concrete casting in Greece.

As a result, the house is a huge concrete cast that acts as a protection/wrap for its interior. The cast was resolved down to the finest detail as there was no room for error. One tiny mistake, a few centimetres out, would have resulted in the displacement of every other element.

All the materials used are exposed, their unfinished state being visible both inside and out. The arrangement of the spaces is based on two geometries: one that follows the site and carries the public areas, another towards the south carrying the bedrooms.

The house comprises a vertical arrangement of individual areas for the children and horizontal common-use areas and defined private zones.

ADDRESS 8 Dexameni Street, Drosia
CLIENT Yiannis Vasiloudis
SIZE 550 square metres
COST 150 million drachmas
BUS 508
ACCESS none

Maria Kaltsa 1991

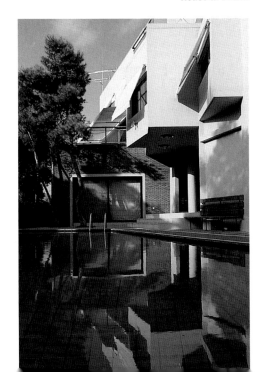

Two houses in Dionysos

The houses, owned by the same person, are situated in a relatively new residential area on an elongated site. Although both houses make use of the same materials and elements and share the courtyard – developed over two levels to correspond to the ground and basement levels of the two homes – they differ in shape and height.

The choice of materials – mainly exposed reinforced concrete, brick and steel – was based on maintenance costs, their resistance to weather conditions, and colour. All materials are left in their natural state, following an approach initiated by the well-known Greek architect Konstantinidis.

ADDRESS 17 Platonos Street, Dionysos
CLIENT George and Helen Arhontidou
ENGINEER Y Tsopanakis, M Philippidis
SIZE 550 square metres (both houses)
COST 130 million drachmas
BUS A7, 536, 550
ACCESS none

Marathon to Ekali

D Issaias, G Makris, G Kalavrytinou, T Papaioannou 1995

D Issaias, G Makris, G Kalavrytinou, T Papaioannou 1995

Ekali residence

Situated in a high-class suburb north of Athens, this modernist two-level house forms a right-angled prism. It is designed around an interior staircase beneath a pyramid-shaped lightwell. The whole house has a definite cubist feel, with interpenetrating geometrical volumes creating intricate spaces and gaps within a preconceived cubist framework.

Well worth visiting.

ADDRESS 77 Thetidos and Prometheos Street, Ekali
COLLABORATING ARCHITECT M Kafritsa
BUS A7, 507, 508, 550
ACCESS none

Tasos Biris and Dimitris Biris 1975

Tasos Biris and Dimitris Biris 1975

Single-family house in Ekali

There is no point visiting this house unless you have made an appointment with the owner – nothing can be seen without going beyond the locked gates. You have been warned.

Hidden behind the large overgrown trees that separate it from the street, this single-family house consists of eight rooms organised horizontally and vertically around a two-storey entrance hall. The orthogonal organisation of the house is emphasised by clearly defined visual axes, complemented by the radial arrangement of the internal spaces through the use of asymmetrical staircases. The central area, the culmination of the hierarchical organisation of the house, acts as a measure and a reference point for the rest of the internal spaces. All the main rooms meet in the central area, along a vertical axis represented both physically and symbolically by the fireplace on the ground floor and the skylight in the roof.

ADDRESS 3 Persefonis Street, Narcissos, Ekali
ENGINEER Jannis Moatsos
SIZE 150 square metres
COST 8 million drachmas
BUS A7, 550, 507, 508
ACCESS by arrangement with owner

Frosso Pimenides 1985

Frosso Pimenides 1985

House in Ekali

The brief called for two types of space: service areas and the living area. The architect used the former as a buffer zone to isolate the rest of the house from the noise of the street, leaving only the garage in direct contact. For the same reason, the façade facing the street has few openings, whereas the south-facing façade has large openings on to the garden down its entire length. The elevations are an attempt to express not only the functions of the building, but also the transition from outdoors to an enclosed space.

The concept of mutation and growth, taken from the environment, also influenced the design of the seating, cupboards and bookcases, giving them dual uses and extra functions.

ADDRESS 24 A Papagou Street, Ekali
COLLABORATING ARCHITECT A Tzonis
BUS A5, 536, 550
ACCESS none

Nikos Kalogeras 1966

Nikos Kalogeras 1966

Nea Penteli

Two-family house in Nea Penteli

This two-family house, on a steep slope of the Penteli hillside, was built around a courtyard created on the south-east side, with interconnecting terraces and verandas.

The smaller part, a one-bedroom house, is orientated towards the courtyard and focuses on a curved wall which creates an intermediate space between the entrance, the kitchen and the living/dining room. The wall turns into a corridor which isolates the more private areas from the rest of the house.

The larger part, a two-bedroom house, sits directly on top with a balcony overlooking the courtyard and steps down to it. Another staircase leads to the upper-level bedrooms and the roof terrace, which takes advantage of the interesting view to the south.

Carefully selected materials and the use of colour successfully preserve the individuality of the two houses yet create an overall impression of visual cohesion.

ADDRESS 19 Konstantinoupoleos Street, Nea Penteli
CLIENT A Tsipopoulos
ENGINEER Y Tsangarakis (civil)
SIZE 245 square metres
COST 35 million drachmas
BUS 423, 550
ACCESS none

Nea Penteli

Tassis Papaioannou and Dimitris Issaias 1992

Tassis Papaioannou and Dimitris Issaias 1992

Nea Penteli house

The building houses a five-member family, and an elderly couple (the parents) in a self-contained apartment. It rests on a sloping site and develops over three levels facing towards the best view. The projecting window frames block the intense light, frame certain views and give this otherwise simple design its distinct island character. The shutters are on the inside of the house and fit exactly into the recess. Vertical open channels carved into the walls of the building collect the rainwater that runs down from the roof.

ADDRESS Salaminomahon Street, Nea Penteli
CLIENT George Giorgantas
COLLABORATING ARCHITECT A Christodoulou
SIZE 280 square metres
COST 3 million drachmas
BUS 423, 442, 450
ACCESS none

Seva Karakosta 1981

Nea Penteli

Seva Karakosta 1981

Pippas residence

The design of this house is based on the theme of symbiosis and isolation, a home within a home. In this case, what brings these two contradictory terms together is the concept of movement – manifested as corridors, stairs and an internal street with axes leading to spaces used by either the family or guests. Marble and ceramic tiles cover the surface of this route through the house, their discreetly changing colours implying variations in movement and use.

Nea Penteli

ADDRESS Aghias Sofias Street, Kato Myrtia, Nea Penteli
CLIENT Pippas
ENGINEER A Athanasiades (civil)
CERAMICS Elena Vernadaki
SIZE 365 square metres
COST 70 million drachmas
BUS 423, 442, 450
ACCESS none

Atelier 66 (D and S Antonakaki) 1988

Nea Penteli

Atelier 66 (D and S Antonakaki) 1988

Kifisia, Kefalari, Politeia

House in Politeia

The design of this house evolved from the need to accommodate an extended family of five and the grandparents. Ramps were carefully positioned at key points in the house to assist the elderly couple and also to unify the three seating areas: in the basement and on the ground floor and upper level.

The building is a simple rectangle within which each function is designated a specific area. This frugality is emphasised by the use of materials in their natural state – exposed reinforced concrete, brick and so on.

ADDRESS Esopou and Pindarou Streets, Politeia
CLIENT George Dokianakis
ENGINEER D Kondis
SIZE 400 square metres
COST 60 million drachmas
BUS A7, 524, 550
ACCESS none

Elias Papayiannopoulos 1986

Elias Papayiannopoulos 1986

Anyfantis residence

This white, modernist building, resting on a small narrow site, is the permanent residence of a four-member family. The architect created a T-shaped design spread over two levels in order to save as many trees as possible and allow breathing space around the three main sides of the building. Visual connection with the trees and the opening up of smaller spaces was achieved through glazed full-height openings and skylights.

The ground floor accommodates the two-level living area, a fireplace, a small WC and a kitchen which opens out to a veranda and which can be isolated from the living room. A metal staircase from the centre of the living room leads to the private spaces of the level above. Here, warm beige and white walls contrast with the red door and skylight frames to create an instant change of atmosphere.

Kifisia, Kefalari, Politeia

ADDRESS 10 Elpidos Street, Strofili, Nea Kifisia
CLIENTS Anna and Yiannis Anyfantis
ENGINEERS M Christofides (structural), G Karayiannis (civil)
COST 3 million drachmas
BUS B7, 505
ACCESS none

Yiannis Anyfantis 1980

Yiannis Anyfantis 1980

Goumas residence

The site accommodates three houses on two levels, arranged in an L-shape with its corner facing north. The outer side of this arrangement, clad with a greyish-white marble, has a minimum amount of openings and provides protection for the swimming pool and garden. All three buildings, which gradually change in height and width, enjoy the view towards the garden through the large glazed openings that dominate the inner side of the L.

Each of the three homes has a kitchen, a living room and two bathrooms on the ground floor, and three bedrooms, two bathrooms and a seating area on the first floor. Shared auxiliary spaces, garages and a gym are in the basement. All rooms are painted white; floors on the lower levels are covered with grey granite, those on the upper levels with oak.

Kifisia, Kefalari, Politeia

ADDRESS 7 Orfeos and Pentelis
Street, Kefalari, Kifisia
CLIENTS Maria and Leonidas Goumas
ENGINEERS George Sifakis (civil),
George Christofides (mechanical)
SIZE 1583 square metres (all three)
COST 800 million drachmas
BUS 509, 526, 550
ACCESS none

Nikos Lykoudis, Ismeni Papaspiliopoulou 1991

Pentelis Street housing block

The work of husband and wife team Helen and George Manetas is never based on great concepts, just on the need to address and satisfy people's basic everyday needs – which are all too often ignored these days. In the design of this housing block they take on this task, usually fulfilled by commercial mass housing, by using the elements and spatial arrangements that they consider most people would appreciate.

Comfortable and bright double volumes, interior spaces which extend outwards to form balconies, outdoor spaces and different levels all come together to create distinctive home environments. Certain volumes, elements and surfaces are combined to provide gradual changes in scale which are then coloured in, echoing the overall composition.

The sensitivity with which the architects have handled and combined these features, using simple but luxurious materials to ensure individuality and variety, leaves the client with a sense of identity, self-respect and a real home. The housing block on Pentelis Street constitutes one of the best examples of the Manetas' theory, delivered as only they know how.

Kifisia, Kefalari, Politeia

ADDRESS Pentelis Street, Kifisia
ENGINEER G Kritikos
CONTRACTOR D Kritikos
SIZE 875 square metres
COST 160 million drachmas
BUS A5, 550 to Kifisia, then a ten-minute walk
ACCESS none

Helen and George Manetas 1994

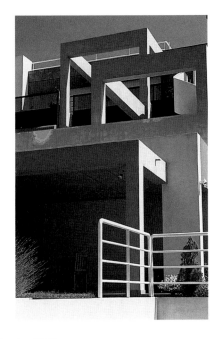

Kifisia, Kefalari, Politeia

Helen and George Manetas 1994

Lianantonakis residence

'How do you imagine your house?' was all the architects asked Lianantonakis, a children's psychiatrist, in order to draw up an original brief. 'A very basic house, like the ones children draw, with a pitched roof and a bent chimney with smoke coming out' was the reply. The architects explained that such houses do not exist, or only in what Jung called an 'archetypal' image. The client also wanted a 'house within a house', a self-contained area for the parents away from the kids, and a small independent summer house at the back for their aunt, with a connecting door to the main house.

To provide a better sense of scale, the architects covered each space with a monopitch roof rather than placing the whole house under a single roof. As the site was extremely small and it was not always possible to take advantage of the surrounding views, a special garden view was created. The portico, with two separate gates leading to the garden and the main entrance, became a transitional space between the street and the house – an element used in ancient Greek architecture.

The house is well liked in the neighbourhood for its changes in scale and discreet nature, and for the clever use of a small site.

ADDRESS 20 Karaiskaki Street, Kifisia
CLIENT Lianantonakis
ENGINEER A Hatzopoulos
CONTRACTOR P Pazianos
SIZE 375 square metres
COST 13 million drachmas
BUS A7, 550
ACCESS none

Kifisia, Kefalari, Politeia

Helen and George Manetas 1980

Helen and George Manetas 1980

Euboea

Modern villa

Only an hour away from Athens (including a boat trip to the island of Euboea, plus a 20-minute walk to the small seafront outpost of Aghios Dimitrios) is this beautiful modern villa, a holiday home for two architects. It is positioned some distance away from the sea to take advantage of the panoramic view out over the water to the rising hills around the almost enclosed bay.

The first phase took two years to build. What I find most interesting is seeing how various elements are added every year. The scheme focuses on a series of external rooms, created in response to the sun's path, prevailing wind currents and the natural landscape as well as the family's needs.

Local materials and traditional methods of building were abandoned in favour of a concrete-frame construction and weatherproof, aluminium fenestration. Little harmony or dialogue exists between built form, contained space and landscape. In an attempt to re-evaluate how to build such a house, a synthesis was sought between the natural and the synthetic, the organic and the abstract, contained space and framed view.

The villa's positioning creates a constricted route from the water's edge through a sequence of built elements – a pier, a garage/bathing deck, a series of outside/inside rooms – and back into the landscape. The formal front façade addresses the villa's abstract relationship with the outside world. To the side, a curved and canted dry-stone wall made from stones found on the site responds to a natural indentation in the landscape and a line of three olive trees.

ADDRESS Aghios Dimitrios, Euboea
CLIENTS Steve McAdam and Christina Norton
ACCESS limited

Steve McAdam and Christina Norton 1990-

Euboea

Steve McAdam and Christina Norton 1990-

Vacation house

This house consists of two bedrooms, a sitting room and two relatively independent guest houses. A relationship between these spaces was established by connecting the two-storey sitting room with the upper-floor bedroom area via a bridge over the central atrium and a staircase linking the bedrooms with the garden. The guest rooms are directly under the bedrooms, with the atrium acting as a meeting place for people staying in the house.

The materials used were exposed reinforced concrete for the main body of the house, iroko-type timber for the door frames, window frames and bedroom floorboards, and tiles from Pilion for other floor surfaces. The walls surrounding the swimming pool are made of stones from Grammatikon (Attica).

ADDRESS on Eretria–Aliveri coastal road, Euboea
CLIENT Manousos Grillakis
ENGINEERS Pagonis, Chroneas
SIZE 350 square metres
COST 55 million drachmas
BUS intercity bus from Athens to Aliveri (end of Aharnon Street), get off at the Holiday Inn stop
ACCESS none

Euboea

Elias Papayiannopoulos 1988

Elias Papayiannopoulos 1988

House at Oxylithos

The house is difficult to find as it is isolated on a steep hill between the village of Oxylithos to the north and the sea to the east. As an indication of just how remote this location is, the house could not be supplied with either water or electricity. A cistern had to be built and portable gas equipment installed.

The spaces are grouped in three zones of open and semi-enclosed areas which run parallel to the slope, away from the violent east wind. A large door is placed on the eastern side to protect the central zone, creating a new daytime living space in more benign weather conditions.

Euboea

ADDRESS Oxylithos, Euboea
CLIENT Zannas
ADVISOR Dimitris Fatouros
ACCESS none

Atelier 66 (D and S Antonakaki) 1978

House at Mytika

This cubist-style house consists of two main triangular elements (in two shades of red) which divide the plan into two spaces that incorporate both exterior and interior areas. The plan derives from a square, the diagonal of which acts as the backbone of the general arrangement. Horizontal and vertical movements originate from here, while the cross-ventilation of the house is achieved through this diagonal on a north–south axis. The interior spaces, spread over three layers, extend out on to balconies which are carved into the mass of the exterior walls. The embodiment of the balconies into the building's general outline creates a variety of shades and thus adds another layer to the abstraction of the composition.

ADDRESS on main Mytika–Halkidas highway, Euboea
CLIENT Yannis Papadopoulos
ENGINEERS Alexis Papaodiseas, Spyros Malides
CONTRUCTOR Ioannis Deligiorgis
SIZE 180 square metres
ACCESS none

Euboea

Angelos Altsitzoglou and Yannis Koukis 1986

Euboea

Angelos Altsitzoglou and Yannis Koukis 1986

Kalfa residence

The outline of this building is not determined by a dividing line defining interior and exterior space. It expands to embody the building's mass and the exit and entry points that correspond with the balconies. This creates an ambiguous space, characteristic of Greek architecture since ancient times. The solid wall dominating the design is punctured at specific points to take advantage of the climatic conditions and the brilliant light of the Greek landscape.

ADDRESS on main Mytika–Halkidas highway, Euboea
CLIENT Mata Kalfa
ENGINEERS Alexis Papaodiseas, Spyros Malides
CONTRUCTOR Ioannis Deligiorgis
SIZE 180 square metres
ACCESS none

Euboea

Angelos Altsitzoglou and Yannis Koukis 1986

Euboea

Angelos Altsitzoglou and Yannis Koukis 1986

Index

Athens: a guide to recent architecture

Athens: a guide to recent architecture

Athens: a guide to recent architecture

Athens: a guide to recent architecture

Athens: a guide to recent architecture

The pictures listed below are reproduced by kind permission of the architects except where otherwise noted. All other pictures are by Errica Protestou.

page 20 Megaron Musices, page 23, page 31, page 37, page 39, page 41, page 43, page 47, page 49, page 59 (photograph by Thomopoulos Konstantinos), page 63, page 69, page 7, page 73, page 77, page 81, page 83, page 87, page 89, pages 90, 91, page 103, page 105, page 107, page 109, page 111 (photograph by Costas Kolokythas), page 113, page 115, page 117, page 131, page 137, pages 144, 145, page 147, pages 148, 149, page 151, page 153, page 155, page 157, page 159, page 161, page 163, page 165, page 171, page 173, page 185, page 187, page 199, pages 205, 207, page 213 (photograph by Thomopoulos Konstantinos), page 215, page 217, page 219, page 221, page 223, page 225, pages 226, 227, page 229, pagw 231, page 237, page 241 (photograph by Panayiotopoulos), page 245, pages 248, 249, page 253, page 257, page 259, page 261, page 263, page 265.